# Financial Literacy Essentials

by Eric Tyson, MBA
with Ray Brown, Bob Carlson,
Robert S. Griswold MSBA CRE CPM,
and Margaret Atkins Munro EA



for dummies®
A Wiley Brand

## Financial Literacy Essentials For Dummies®

Published by: **John Wiley & Sons, Inc.**, 111 River Street, Hoboken, NJ 07030-5774, www.wiley.com



Published simultaneously in Canada



For general information on our other products and services, please contact our Customer Care Department within the U.S. at 877-762-2974, outside the U.S. at 317-572-3993, or fax 317-572-4002. For technical support, please visit https://hub.wiley.com/community/support/dummies.

Wiley publishes in a variety of print and electronic formats and by print-on-demand. Some material included with standard print versions of this book may not be included in e-books or in print-on-demand. If this book refers to media that is not included in the version you purchased, you may download this material at http://booksupport.wiley.com. For more information about Wiley products, visit www.wiley.com.

Library of Congress Control Number: 2025933227

ISBN 978-1-394-32616-7 (pbk); ISBN 978-1-394-32618-1 (ePDF);
ISBN 978-1-394- 32617-4 (epub)

SKY10101816_040325

# Table of Contents

# Introduction

Possessing financial literacy helps you understand the relationship between the money you earn, the money you save and spend, and the money you invest. With this knowledge, you can make informed financial decisions to meet your short- and long-term financial goals.

You may want to buy a home, plan to finance a child's higher education, retire and travel the world by a certain age, or all these things and more. Because you understand the basics of how money works, you can create an effective financial strategy toward meeting these goals.

Part of increasing your financial literacy requires considering your own experience with money. Although you can't change what the educational system and your parents did or didn't teach you about personal finances, you now have the ability to find out what you need to know to manage your finances. Reading this book is a good place to start.

## About This Book

This book helps you develop a basic understanding of financial literacy. Aside from being packed with updated information, another great feature of this book is that you can read it from cover to cover if you want, or you can read a particular chapter or part without having to read what comes before it. Handy cross-references direct you to other places in the book for more details on a particular subject.

## Foolish Assumptions

In writing this book, I have assumed that you want to learn the basics of financial literacy while also receiving expert advice about important financial topics (such as paying off and reducing the cost of debt, planning for major goals, making wise investments). I also assume that you want quality information and answers presented as efficiently as possible.

## Icons Used in This Book

The icons in this book help you find particular kinds of information that may be useful to you.

TIP

This target flags strategy recommendations for making the most of your money.

REMEMBER

This icon points out information that you'll definitely want to remember.

WARNING

This icon marks things to avoid and points out common mistakes people make when managing their finances.

## Where to Go from Here

This book is organized so you can go wherever you want to find complete information. Want to read about investing strategies, for example? Go to Chapter 5 for that. Feel the urge to get your insurance needs in order or to check on what type of insurance you really need? Head to Chapter 8. You also can check out the table of contents to find broad categories of information and a chapter-by-chapter rundown of what this book offers, or you can look up a specific topic in the index.

If you're not sure where you want to go, you may want to start at the beginning with Chapter 1. It gives you all the basic info you need to assess your financial literacy and points to places where you can find more detailed information for improving it.

IN THIS CHAPTER

» **Understanding the basics of financial literacy**

» **Identifying hurdles to financial success**

» **Recognizing and avoiding bad advice and information**

» **Avoiding common money mistakes**

# Chapter 1 Introduction to Financial Literacy

Personal finance involves much more than managing and investing money. It also includes making all the pieces of your financial life fit together; it means lifting yourself out of financial illiteracy.

This chapter introduces the basics of financial literacy. It explains why possessing financial literacy helps pave the road to financial success and some pitfalls you may encounter along the way.

## What Is Financial Literacy, Anyway?

To be literate in personal finance, you need to get a handle on these topics:

» **Managing your everyday transactions:** Accounting for money that passes through your hands and your transaction accounts in the short term

- **Investing for the long term:** Knowing the best ways to invest money for better returns and longer-term purposes
- **Protecting your money:** Protecting your income and assets with insurance

## Budgeting and transaction accounts

If you're like most people, as you earn money, much of it too quickly passes through your hands or, more specifically, into and out of your transaction accounts. In addition, a hefty chunk of money you earn is siphoned off to federal, state, and local taxes. What's left is used to pay your monthly living expenses, such as housing, food, utilities, clothing, and hopefully for some entertainment and recreation.

Managing your monthly living expenses (including taxes) and budget and establishing and working toward financial goals takes time and effort. Chapter 2 describes the basics of creating a budget and tracking expenses.

## Investing

When you're spending less than you earn and able to save new money each month, you have the pleasant but challenging problem of deciding where and when to invest your savings. Or maybe you already have additional money you want to invest and make work harder for you.

The world of investments is complicated and filled with pitfalls. That contributes to some folks leaving their excess money sitting in their low-interest transaction accounts by default. While you could do worse (by losing money in poor investments), you can certainly do better — and you probably need to do better in order to accomplish your financial goals. Chapter 5 covers investing and helps you grasp the essentials of that important task.

## Insurance

When you're earning money and have some assets (for example, a car, house, and so on), insurance protects against the loss of that income and your assets. If others are dependent upon your employment income, you likely need some life insurance. Even without dependents, you're probably dependent on your own income and thus should have adequate disability insurance.

Assets like a car and home require sufficient insurance protection. And, as your investments and net worth grow, having some excess liability insurance makes sense as well. See Chapter 8 for important details on insurance.

## Why It Matters: The Power of Knowing Your Money Stuff

Understanding the relationship between the money you earn, the money you save and spend, and the money you invest helps you make informed financial decisions to meet your short- and long-term financial goals.

Think about where your parents learned about money management, and then consider whether they had the time, energy, or inclination to research choices before making their decisions. For example, if they didn't do enough research or had faulty information, your parents may mistakenly have thought that banks were the best places for investing money or that buying stocks was like going to Las Vegas. (You can find out more about where to invest your money in Chapter 5.)

TIP

If you have children of your own, don't underestimate their potential or send them out into the world without the skills they need to be productive and happy adults. Buy them some good financial books when they head off to college or begin their first job.

### Identifying hurdles to financial success

Perhaps you know that you should live within your means, buy and hold sound investments for the long term, and secure proper insurance coverage; however, you can't bring yourself to do these things. Everyone knows how difficult it is to break problematic habits that have been practiced for many years. The temptation to spend money lurks everywhere. Ads show attractive and popular people enjoying the fruits of their labor — a new car, an exotic vacation, and a lavish home.

Maybe you felt deprived by your tightwad parents as a youngster, or maybe you're bored with life and like the adventure of buying new things. If only you could hit it big on one or two investments, you think, you could get rich quick and do what you really want with your life. As for disasters and catastrophes, well, those things happen to other people, not to you. Besides, you'll probably have advance warning of pending problems, so you can prepare accordingly, right?

Your emotions and temptations can get the better of you. Certainly, part of successfully managing your finances involves coming to terms with your shortcomings and the consequences of your behaviors. If you don't, you may end up enslaved to an unsatisfactory job so that you can keep feeding your spending addiction. Or you may spend more time with your investments than you do with your family and friends. Or unexpected events may leave you reeling financially; disasters and catastrophes can happen to anyone at any time.

REMEMBER

Intelligent personal financial strategies have little to do with your gender, ethnicity, or marital status. All people need to manage their finances wisely. Some aspects of financial management become more or less important at different points in your life, but for the most part, the principles remain the same for everyone.

## Understanding your personal and emotional hurdles

Avoid the psychological trap of blaming something else for your financial problems. For example, some people believe that adult problems can be traced back to childhood and how they were raised. Particular backgrounds certainly can have a negative impact on some people's tendency to make the wrong choices during their lives. Exploring your personal history can yield important clues to what makes you tick. But adults make choices and engage in behaviors that affect themselves as well as others. They shouldn't blame their parents for their own inability to plan for their financial future, live within their means, and make sound investments.

Some people also tend to blame their financial shortcomings on not earning more income. Such people believe that if only they earned more, their financial (and personal) problems would melt away. My experience working and speaking with people from diverse economic backgrounds has taught me that achieving financial success — and more importantly, personal happiness — has much less to do with how much income a person makes but rather much more to do with what they make of what they have. I know financially wealthy people who are emotionally poor even though they have all the material goods they want. Likewise, I know people who are quite happy, content, and emotionally wealthy even though they're struggling financially.

Americans — even those who have not had an "easy" life — ought to be able to come up with numerous things to be happy about and grateful for: a family who loves them; friends who laugh at their stupid jokes; the freedom to catch a movie, play some pickleball, or read a good book; or a great singing voice, a good sense of humor, or a full head of hair.

## Developing good financial habits

To successfully implement an intelligent personal financial strategy, you have to practice good financial habits just as you practice other good habits, such as brushing your teeth or eating a healthy diet and getting some exercise.

Regardless of your income, you can make your dollars stretch further if you practice good financial habits and avoid mistakes, such as the common ones I discuss in Chapter 2. In fact, the lower your income, the more important it is that you make the most of your income and savings (because you don't have the luxury of falling back on your next big paycheck to bail you out).

TIP

Throughout this book, I highlight ways you can overcome temptations and keep control of your money rather than let your emotions and money rule you. As you read, make a short list of your financial marching orders and then start working away.

# How to Avoid the "Oops, I Bought a Timeshare" Scenario

Most folks know that they're not financial geniuses. So they set out to take control of their money matters by reading about personal finance or consulting a financial advisor.

But reading and seeking advice to find out how to manage your money can be dangerous if you're a novice. Misinformation can come from popular and seemingly reliable information sources, as I explain in the following sections.

## Assessing free financial content online

In addition to being able to quickly access what we want, the other major attraction of the internet is the abundance of seemingly free websites providing piles of apparently free content. Appearances, however, can be decidedly deceiving!

While there are exceptions to any rule, the fact of the matter is that the vast majority of websites purporting to provide a seemingly never-ending array of "free" content are rife with conflicts of interest and quality problems due to the following:

- **Advertising:** Any publication that accepts advertising has a potential conflict of interest because it may not want to publish articles that would upset its advertisers. Such a mindset, however, can stand in the way of telling consumers the unvarnished truth about various products and services. For example, credit card companies aren't very interested in advertising someplace that publishes articles highlighting the negatives of credit cards. (Check out the section "Considering the influence of advertising" later in this chapter for more on the power of advertising to influence the financial information you encounter online, on TV, and elsewhere.)
- **Advertorials:** Too many website owners are unwilling or unable to pay real writers for quality content and instead publish articles that are written and provided by advertisers. These pieces of "content" are known as *advertorials* and, in the worst cases, aren't even clearly labeled as advertisements, which is precisely what they are.
- **Affiliate relationships:** Many companies pay "referral fees" to websites that bring in new customers. Here's how that practice causes major conflicts of interest. On a financial website, you read a glowing review of a particular financial product or service. And the site provides a helpful link to the website of the provider of that product or service. Unbeknownst to you, when you click on that link and buy something, the seller kicks money back to the "affiliate" who reeled you in. At a minimum, such relationships should be clearly disclosed and detailed in any review.
- **Insufficient editorial oversight:** At most established, quality print publications, there are usually numerous editors who oversee the publication and all its articles.

This structure helps ensure the accuracy of what gets into print (although bias, such as political bias, isn't necessarily controlled). Unfortunately, the shoestring budget on which many websites operate precludes these quality-control checks and balances. Thus, sites operated by nonexperts proffering advice place you at great risk.

» **Lack of accountability:** In part because of a lack of editorial oversight, there's also often a lack of accountability for advice given online. This situation is especially problematic on the numerous sites that are run without disclosure of who is actually in charge of the site and/or who is writing the articles. Although such anonymity may be helpful to the site and its content providers, it's certainly not in your best interests because it prevents you from checking out the background, qualifications, and track record of the providers.

## Protecting yourself from supposed financial gurus

While new mediums may come while others fade, the same types of dangers continue to trip up people with their money. In this section, I highlight what you can do to protect yourself from being led astray by supposed financial gurus and celebrities.

### Checking professional work experience and education credentials

TIP

Before you take financial advice from anyone, examine their background, including professional work experience and education credentials. This is true whether you're getting advice from an advisor, writer, talk show host, or TV financial reporter.

If you can't easily find such information, that's usually a red flag. People with something to hide or a lack of something redeeming to say about themselves usually don't promote their background.

Of course, just because someone seems to have a relatively impressive-sounding background doesn't mean that they have your best interests in mind or have honestly presented their qualifications.

You can't always accept stated credentials and qualifications at face value, because some people lie (witness the billions lost to hedge fund Ponzi-scheme-man Bernie Madoff). You can't sniff out liars by the way they look, their résumé, their gender, or their age. You can, however, increase your chances of being tipped off by being skeptical (and by regularly reading the "Guru Watch" section of my website at www.erictyson.com).

### Resisting the attraction of celebrity endorsers

Celebrities were used big-time as endorsers in recent years in the problematic cryptocurrency space. You've perhaps heard of the now defunct and bankrupt offshore cryptocurrency exchange FTX, which spent hundreds of millions of dollars on advertising and paying celebrity endorsers like basketball stars Shaquille O'Neil and Stephen Curry, NFL quarterbacks Trevor Lawrence and Tom Brady, comedian Larry David, supermodel Gisele Bündchen, tennis great Naomi Osaka, baseball stars David "Big Papi" Ortiz and Shohei Ohtani, and Shark Tank's Kevin O'Leary.

In some of the advertisements for FTX, the well-paid celebrity endorsers joked about not knowing much about cryptocurrencies but then suggested that that was why they used FTX, implying that FTX was the expert. In other ads, some celebrities acted like they were calling friends to ask if they too were "in" to invest through FTX. Lawyers have filed a class action lawsuit against the celebrities for being bought off, failing to disclose large endorsement fees, and misleading the public to invest billions of dollars in FTX, which turned out to be a fraud.

Always remember that celebrities may have a talent that brings them notoriety, fame, and fortune, but they are no smarter than anyone else when it comes to their personal finances. Furthermore, and too often, they have enormous (and rarely well disclosed) conflicts of interest in what they tout.

### Watching for outrageous performance claims

You can see a number of hucksters for what they are by using common sense in reviewing some of their outrageous claims.

Some sources of advice lure you in by promising outrageous returns. The stock market has generated average annual returns of about 9 percent over the long term. The perils of following an approach that advocates short-term trading (as an example) with the allure of high profits are numerous:

» You'll rack up enormous brokerage commissions.

» On occasions where your short-term trades produce a profit, you'll pay high ordinary income-tax rates rather than the far lower capital gains rate for investments held more than 12 months.

» You won't make big profits — quite the reverse. If you stick with this approach, you'll underperform the market averages.

» You'll make yourself a nervous wreck. This type of trading is gambling, not investing. Get sucked up in it, and you'll lose more than money — you may also lose the love and respect of your family and friends.

## Considering the influence of advertising

WARNING

Thousands of publications and media outlets — websites, blogs, podcasts, radio, TV, magazines, and even some newspapers — dole out personal financial advice and perspectives. Although some of these "service providers" collect revenue from subscribers, virtually all are dependent — in some cases, fully dependent (especially the internet, radio, and TV) — on advertising dollars. Although advertising is a necessary part of capitalism, advertisers can taint and, in some cases, dictate the content of what you read, listen to, and view.

Be sure to consider how dependent a publication or media outlet is on advertising. I find that "free" publications, websites/blogs, podcasts, radio, and TV are the ones that most often create conflicts of interest by pandering to advertisers. (All derive all their revenue from advertising.)

Much of what's on the internet is advertiser-driven as well. Many of the investing sites on the internet offer advice about individual stocks. Interestingly, such sites derive much of their revenue from online brokerage firms seeking to recruit customers.

Keep in mind that you have virtually zero privacy on "free" websites because they make money by selling access to website visitors like you to companies and people with something to sell.

As you read various publications, watch TV, or listen to podcasts and radio, note how consumer-oriented these media are.

Do you get the feeling that they're looking out for your interests? For example, if lots of auto manufacturers advertise, does the media outlet ever tell you how to save money when shopping for a car or the importance of buying a car within your means? Or are they primarily creating an advertiser-friendly broadcast or publication?

## Preventing Common Money Mistakes

Financial problems, like many medical problems, are best detected early. And as with your personal health, the best "problems" are those avoided — clean living is a good thing, right? Here are the common personal financial problems I've seen in my work as a financial counselor:

- **Not planning:** Most of us procrastinate. That's why we have deadlines (like April 15) — and deadline extensions (need another six months to get that tax return done?). Unfortunately, you may have no explicit deadlines with your personal finances. You can allow your credit card debt to accumulate, or you can leave your savings sitting in lousy investments for years. You can pay higher taxes, leave gaps in your retirement and insurance coverage, and overpay for financial products. Of course, planning your finances isn't as much fun as planning a vacation, but doing the former can help you take more of the latter. See Chapter 7 for details on setting financial goals.
- **Overspending:** Simple arithmetic helps you determine that savings is the difference between what you earn and what you spend (assuming that you're not spending more than you're earning!). To increase your savings, you either have to work more, increase your earning power through education or job advancement, get to know a wealthy family who wants to leave its fortune to you, or spend less. For most people, especially over the short term, the thrifty approach is the key to building savings and wealth.
- **Buying with consumer credit:** Carrying a debt balance from month to month on your credit card or buying a car on credit means that even more of your future earnings are going to be earmarked for debt repayment. Buying on credit, including the recent trend of "Buy Now, Pay Later,"

encourages you to spend more than you can really afford. Chapter 4 discusses debt and credit problems.

- **Delaying saving for financial independence/retirement:** Most folks say that they want to achieve financial independence/retire by their mid-60s or sooner. But to accomplish this goal, they need to save a reasonable chunk (around 10 percent) of their incomes starting sooner rather than later. The longer you wait to start saving for retirement, the harder reaching your goal will be. And you'll pay much more in taxes to boot if you don't take advantage of the tax benefits of investing through particular retirement savings accounts. For information on planning for retirement, see Chapter 7.
- **Falling prey to financial sales pitches:** Steer clear of people who pressure you to make decisions, promise you high investment returns, and lack the proper training and experience to help you. Supposed great deals that can't wait for a little reflection or a second opinion are often disasters waiting to happen. A sucker may be born every minute, but a slick salesperson is pitching something every second! For important investment concepts and which kinds of investments to avoid, turn to Chapter 5.
- **Not doing your homework:** To get the best deal, shop around, read reviews, and get advice from objective third parties. You also need to check references and track records so that you don't hire incompetent, self-serving, or fraudulent financial advisors. (For more on hiring financial planners, see Chapter 10.)
- **Making decisions based on emotion:** You're most vulnerable to making the wrong moves financially after a major life change (a job loss, divorce, or death in the family, for example) or when you feel pressure. Maybe your investments plunged in value. Or perhaps a recent divorce has you fearing that you won't be able to afford to retire when you planned, so you pour thousands of dollars into some newfangled financial product. Take your time and keep your emotions out of decisions.
- **Not separating the wheat from the chaff:** In any field in which you're not an expert, you are at risk of following the advice of someone you think is an expert but really isn't. This book shows you how to separate the financial fluff from the

financial facts. You are the person who is best able to manage your personal finances. Educate and trust yourself!

- **Exposing yourself to catastrophic risk:** You're vulnerable if you and your family don't have insurance to pay for financially devastating losses. In the worst cases, folks without a savings reserve and a support network can end up homeless. Many people lack sufficient insurance coverage to replace their income. Don't wait for a tragedy to strike to find out whether you have the right insurance coverage. Check out Chapter 8 for more on insurance.
- **Focusing too much on money:** Placing too much emphasis on making and saving money can warp your perspective on what's important in life. Money is not the first — or even second — priority in happy people's lives. Your health, relationships with family and friends, career satisfaction, and fulfilling interests are more significant. That's not to say that it's okay to ignore or give insufficient attention to your personal finances and associated decisions.

REMEMBER

**Money problems can be fixed over time with changes in your behavior. This book helps you gain the financial literacy you need to build habits to address any money problems you have and avoid developing money problems in the future.**

IN THIS CHAPTER

» Making a budget

» Tracking what you spend

» Calculating your savings rate

» Determining your financial net worth

» Planning for emergencies

# Chapter 2 Budgeting Basics

Creating a budget may sound like a daunting task, but it doesn't have to be. In fact, it's a great way to get a leg up on your savings so that you have the future funds to pay for the things you want.

This chapter shows you how to create a budget and provides the tools you need to track what you spend, calculate your savings rate, determine your financial net worth, and plan for common financial emergencies that you may encounter along the way.

## Creating a Budget

When most people hear the word *budgeting*, they think unpleasant thoughts — like those associated with *dieting* — and rightfully so. But budgeting can help you move from knowing how much you spend on various things to successfully reducing your spending.

The first step in the process of *budgeting*, or planning your future spending, is to analyze where your current spending is going. After you do that, calculate how much more you'd like to save each month. Then comes the hard part: deciding where to make cuts in your spending.

Suppose that you're currently not saving any of your monthly income and you want to save 10 percent for retirement. If you can save and invest through a tax-sheltered retirement account — for example, a 401(k), 403(b), or a SEP-IRA — you don't actually need to cut your spending by 10 percent to reach a savings goal of 10 percent (of your gross income). When you contribute money to a tax-deductible retirement account, you reduce your federal and state taxes. If you're a moderate income earner paying, say, 30 percent in federal and state taxes on your marginal income, you actually need to reduce your spending by only 7 percent to save 10 percent. The other 3 percent of the savings comes from the lowering of your taxes. (The higher your tax bracket, the less you need to cut your spending to reach a particular savings goal. To find your tax bracket, see Chapter 9.)

So to boost your savings rate to 10 percent, go through your current spending category by category until you come up with enough proposed cuts to reduce your spending by 7 percent. Make your cuts in the areas that will be the least painful and where you're getting the least value from your current level of spending. (If you don't have access to a tax-deductible retirement account, budgeting still involves the same process of assessment and making cuts in various spending categories, but your cuts need to add up to the entire amount you want to save, in this example, 10 percent rather than 7 percent.)

Another method of budgeting involves starting completely from scratch rather than examining your current expenses and making cuts from that starting point. Ask yourself how much you'd like to spend on different categories. The advantage of this approach is that it doesn't allow your current spending levels to constrain your thinking. You'll likely be amazed at the discrepancies between what you think you should be spending and what you actually are spending in certain categories.

## Tracking Expenses: From Lattes to Rent

Most folks should be tracking their spending. The one category of people I would exempt from needing to monitor (categorize) where their money goes are those who are satisfied with the portion of their income they're able to save and who are saving enough to accomplish their goals. In this section, I provide some guidelines and frameworks for tracking your spending and getting a handle on overspending.

## Tracking spending the "low-tech" way

Analyzing your spending is a little bit like being a detective. Your goal is to reconstruct the spending. You probably have some major clues at your fingertips or somewhere on the desk or computer where you handle your finances.

TIP

Unless you keep meticulous records that detail every dollar you spend, you won't have perfect information. Don't sweat it! A number of sources can enable you to detail where you've been spending your money. To get started, get out/access your

- Recent pay stubs
- Recent tax returns (federal and state)
- Online banking/bill payment record
- Log of checks paid and monthly debit-card transactions
- Credit- and charge-card bills and transactions

Ideally, you want to assemble the information needed to track 12 months of spending. But if your spending patterns don't fluctuate greatly from month to month (or you won't complete the exercise if it means compiling a year's worth of data), you can reduce your data gathering to one six-month period, or to every second or third month for the past year. If you take a major vacation or spend a large amount on gifts during certain months of the year, make sure that you include these months in your analysis. Also account for insurance or other payments that you may choose not to pay monthly and instead pay quarterly, semiannually, or annually.

TIP

Purchases made with cash are the hardest to track because they don't leave a paper trail. Over the course of a week or perhaps even a month, you *could* keep a record of everything you buy with cash. Tracking cash can be an enlightening exercise, but it can also be tedious. (See the section "Tracking your spending on 'free' websites and apps" later in this chapter.) If you lack the time and patience, you can try *estimating*. Think about a typical week or month — how often do you buy things with cash? For example, if you eat lunch out four days a week, paying around

$8 per meal, that's about $130 a month. You may also want to try adding up all the cash withdrawals from your checking account statement (or any other account from which you do cash transactions) and then working backward to try to remember where you spent the cash.

Separate your expenditures into as many useful and detailed categories as possible. Table 2-1 gives you a suggested format; you can tailor it to fit your needs. Remember, if you lump too much of your spending into broad, meaningless categories like "Other," you'll end up right back where you started — wondering where all the money went. (*Note:* When completing the tax section in Table 2-1, report the total tax you paid for the year as tabulated on your annual income-tax return — and take the total Social Security and Medicare taxes paid from your end-of-year pay stub — rather than the tax withheld or paid during the year.)

**TABLE 2-1 Detailing Your Spending**

| Category | Monthly Average ($) | Percent of Total Gross Income (%) |
|---|---|---|
| **Taxes, taxes, taxes (income)** | | ______ |
| FICA (Social Security & Medicare) | ______ | |
| Federal | ______ | |
| State and local | ______ | |
| **The roof over your head** | | ______ |
| Rent | ______ | |
| Mortgage | ______ | |
| Property taxes | ______ | |
| Gas/electric/oil | ______ | |
| Water/garbage | ______ | |
| Phones | ______ | |
| Cable TV, streaming & internet services | ______ | |

| Category | Monthly Average ($) | Percent of Total Gross Income (%) |
|---|---|---|
| Gardener/housekeeper | ______ | |
| Furniture/appliances | ______ | |
| Maintenance/repairs | ______ | |
| **Food, glorious food** | | ______ |
| Supermarket | ______ | |
| Restaurants and takeout | ______ | |
| **Getting around** | | ______ |
| Gasoline | ______ | |
| Maintenance/repairs | ______ | |
| State registration fees | ______ | |
| Tolls and parking | ______ | |
| Taxi, on-demand car services, rentals | ______ | |
| Bus or subway fares | ______ | |
| **Style** | | ______ |
| Clothing | ______ | |
| Shoes | ______ | |
| Jewelry (watches, earrings) | ______ | |
| Dry-cleaning | ______ | |
| **Debt repayments (excluding mortgage)** | | ______ |
| Credit/charge cards | ______ | |
| Auto loans | ______ | |
| Student loans | ______ | |
| Other | ______ | |

*(continued)*

**TABLE 2-1** ***(continued)***

| Category | Monthly Average ($) | Percent of Total Gross Income (%) |
|---|---|---|
| **Fun stuff** | | ______ |
| Entertainment (movies, concerts) | ______ | |
| Vacation and travel | ______ | |
| Gifts | ______ | |
| Hobbies | ______ | |
| Subscriptions/memberships | ______ | |
| Pets | ______ | |
| Other | ______ | |
| **Personal care** | | ______ |
| Haircuts | ______ | |
| Health club or gym | ______ | |
| Makeup | ______ | |
| Other | ______ | |
| **Personal business** | | ______ |
| Accountant/attorney/financial advisor | ______ | |
| Other | ______ | |
| **Healthcare** | | ______ |
| Physicians and hospitals | ______ | |
| Drugs | ______ | |
| Dental and vision | ______ | |
| Therapy | ______ | |
| **Insurance** | | ______ |
| Homeowner's/renter's | ______ | |
| Auto | ______ | |

| Category | Monthly Average ($) | Percent of Total Gross Income (%) |
|---|---|---|
| Health | ______ | |
| Life | ______ | |
| Disability | ______ | |
| Long-term care | ______ | |
| Umbrella liability | ______ | |
| **Educational expenses** | | ______ |
| Tuition | ______ | |
| Books | ______ | |
| Supplies | ______ | |
| Housing costs (room & board) | ______ | |
| **Children** | | ______ |
| Day care | ______ | |
| Toys | ______ | |
| Activities | ______ | |
| Child support | ______ | |
| **Charitable donations** | ______ | ______ |
| **Other** | | ______ |
| ______________ | ______ | |
| ______________ | ______ | |
| ______________ | ______ | |

## Tracking your spending on "free" websites and apps

Software programs, apps, and websites can assist you with paying bills and tracking your spending. The main advantage of using these is that you can continually track your spending as long as you keep entering/uploading the information. Such tools can even help speed up the check-writing process (after you figure out how to use them, which isn't always an easy thing to do).

More of these sites keep springing up, but among those you may have heard of and stumbled upon are Budget Tracker, Mint, and Yodlee. I've kicked the tires and checked out these sites, and frankly, I have mixed-to-negative feelings about them. Here are the problems I've found:

- **Conflicts of interest:** Many of these "free" tools are loaded with advertising and/or have *affiliate relationships* with companies. This simply means that these companies get paid if you click on a link to one of their recommended service providers and buy what they are selling. This compensation, of course, creates an enormous conflict of interest and thoroughly taints any recommendation made by "free" sites that profit from affiliate referrals.
- **Privacy and security concerns:** After registering you as a user, the first thing most of these tools want you to do is connect directly to your financial institutions (banks, brokerages, investment companies) and download your investment account and spending data. If your intuition tells you this may not be a good idea, trust your instincts. Yes, there are security concerns, but those pale in comparison to privacy concerns and apprehension about the endless pitching to you of products and services.
- **Oversimplified calculators:** These websites typically offer incredibly simplistic calculators that are too limited to be useful. One that purports to help with retirement planning doesn't allow users to choose a retirement age younger than 62 and has no provisions for part-time work. When it asks about your assets, it makes no distinction between equity in your home and financial assets (stocks, bonds, mutual funds, and so on).
- **No phone support:** These sites generally offer no phone support, so if you encounter a problem using them, you're relegated to ping-ponging emails in the hope of getting your questions answered.

TIP

Paper, pencil, and a calculator can work just fine for tracking your spending. One app that I have reviewed and liked is Goodbudget. For more on that app and others, see Chapter 3.

## Getting a handle on overspending

If you're like most people, you must live within your means to accomplish your financial goals. Doing so requires consistently spending less than you earn and then investing your savings intelligently (unless you plan on winning the lottery or receiving a large inheritance).

This section considers some of the adversaries you're up against as you attempt to control your spending.

### Using and misusing credit

Thanks to ATMs, credit cards, myriad smartphone apps, PayPal, Venmo, and so on, your money is always available, 24/7. Sometimes it may seem as though lenders are trying to give away money by making credit so easily available. But this free money is a dangerous illusion.

Here are the mistakes people tend to make with credit:

- **Making purchases you can't afford:** Credit is most perilous when you make consumption purchases you can't afford in the first place. When it comes to consumer debt (credit cards, auto loans, and the like), lenders aren't giving away anything except the misfortune of getting in over your head, racking up high interest charges, and delaying your progress toward your financial and personal goals.
- **Carrying a balance:** If you pay your bill in full every month, credit cards offer a convenient way to buy things with an interest-free, short-term loan. But if you carry your debt over from month to month at high interest rates, credit cards encourage you to live beyond your means. Credit cards make it easy and tempting to spend money that you don't have.

WARNING

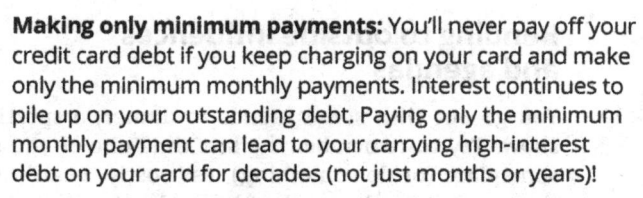

- **Making only minimum payments:** You'll never pay off your credit card debt if you keep charging on your card and make only the minimum monthly payments. Interest continues to pile up on your outstanding debt. Paying only the minimum monthly payment can lead to your carrying high-interest debt on your card for decades (not just months or years)!
- **Paying for insurance services:** Some credit cards sell cardholders "insurance" at a cost of 10 to 15-plus percent

annually to pay the minimum payments due on credit card balances for those months that the debtor is unable to pay because of some life transition event (such as a job layoff). With credit card interest rates around 18 percent on balances, when you add the insurance charges, the total annual interest rate is upward of around 30 percent!

TIP

If you have a knack for charging up a storm and spending more than you should with those little pieces of plastic, only one solution exists: Get rid of your credit cards. You can function without them. (See Chapter 4 for details on how to live without credit cards.)

## Taking out car loans

Walking onto a car lot and going home with a new car that you couldn't afford if you had to pay cash (or wouldn't choose to buy if you did have that much cash) is easy. The dealer gets you thinking in terms of monthly payments that sound small when compared to what that four-wheeler is *really* gonna cost you. Auto loans are easy for just about anyone to get.

WARNING

Car dealers want you to think in terms of monthly payments because the cost *sounds* so cheap: $399 for a car. But, of course, that's $399 per month for many, many months. You're gonna be payin' forever — after all, you just bought a car that cost a huge chunk of your yearly take-home income.

But it gets worse. What does the total sticker price come to when interest charges on borrowed money are added in? (Even if interest charges are low, you may still be buying a car with a sticker price you can't afford.) And what about the cost of insurance, registration, and maintenance over the seven or so years that you'll probably own the car? Now you're probably up to more than a year's worth of your income. Ouch!

## Bending to outside influences and agendas

You go out with some friends to dinner, a sporting event, or a show. Try to remember the last time one of you said, "Let's go someplace (or do something) less costly. I can't afford to spend this much." On the one hand, you don't want to be a stick in the mud. But on the other hand, some of your friends may have more money than you do — and the ones who don't may not be saving money or may be running up debt fast.

When was the last time you heard someone say that they decided to forgo a purchase because they were saving for retirement or a home purchase? It doesn't happen often, does it? Just dealing with the here-and-now and forgetting your long-term needs and goals is tempting. This mindset leads people to toil away for too many years in jobs they dislike.

Living for today has its virtues: Your tomorrow *may* not come. But odds are good that it will. Will you still feel the same way about today's spending decisions tomorrow? Or will you feel guilty that you again failed to stick to your goals?

Your spending habits should be driven by *your* desires and plans, not those of others. If you haven't set any goals yet, you may not know how much you should be saving. Chapter 4 helps you kick-start the planning and saving process.

### Spending to feel good

Life is full of stress, obligations, and demands. "I work hard," you may say, "and darn it, I deserve to indulge!" Especially after your boss took the credit for your most recent great idea or blamed you for their latest screw up. So you buy something expensive or go to a fancy restaurant. Feel better? You probably won't when the bill arrives. And the more you spend, the less you save, and the longer you'll be stuck working for jerks like your boss!

Just as people can become addicted to alcohol, tobacco, television, and the internet, some people also become addicted to the high they get from spending. Researchers can identify a number of psychological causes for a spending addiction, with some relating to how your parents handled money and spending.

If your spending and debt problems are chronic, or even if you'd simply like to be a better consumer and saver, see Chapter 4 for more information.

## Figuring Out Your Savings Rate

How much money have you actually saved in the past year? By that I mean the amount of new money you've added to your nest egg, stash, or whatever you like to call it.

Most people don't know or have only a vague idea of the rate at which they're saving money. The answer may sober, terrify, or pleasantly surprise you. In order to calculate your savings over the past year, you need to calculate your net worth as of today *and* as of one year ago.

The amount you actually saved over the past year is equal to the change in your net worth over the past year — in other words, your net worth today minus your net worth from one year ago. I know it may be a pain to find statements showing what your investments were worth a year ago, but bear with me: It's a useful exercise.

If you own your home, ignore this in the calculations. (However, you can consider the extra payments you make to pay off your mortgage principal faster as new savings.) And don't include personal property and consumer goods, such as your car, computer, clothing, and so on, with your assets. (See the next section "Calculating Your Financial Net Worth" if you need more help with this task.)

When you have your net worth figures from both years, plug them into Step 1 of Table 2-2. If you're anticipating the exercise and are already subtracting your net worth of a year ago from what it is today in order to determine your rate of savings, your instincts are correct, but the exercise isn't quite that simple. You need to do a few more calculations in Step 2 of Table 2-2. Why? Well, counting the appreciation of the investments you've owned over the past year as savings wouldn't be fair. Suppose you bought 100 shares of a stock a year ago at $17 per share, and now the value is $34 per share. Your investment increased in value by $1,700 during the past year. Although you'd be the envy of your friends at the next party if you casually mentioned your investments, the $1,700 of increased value is not "savings." Instead, it represents appreciation on your investments, so you must remove this appreciation from the calculations. (Just so you know, I'm not unfairly penalizing you for your shrewd investments — you also get to add back the decline in value of your less-successful investments.)

TIP

If all this calculating gives you a headache, you get stuck, or you just hate crunching numbers, try the intuitive, seat-of-the-pants approach: Save a regular portion of your monthly income. You can save it in a separate savings or retirement account. For information on tracking your money with technology, turn to Chapter 3.

How much do you save in a typical month? Get out the statements for accounts you contribute to or save money in monthly. It doesn't matter if you're saving money in a retirement account that you can't access — money is money.

**TABLE 2-2 Your Savings Rate over the Past Year**

| Step 1: Figuring your savings | | | |
|---|---|---|---|
| **Today** | | **One Year Ago** | |
| Savings & investments | $______ | Savings & investments | $______ |
| Loans & debts | $______ | Loans & debts | $______ |
| = Net worth today | $______ | = Net worth 1 year ago | $______ |
| **Step 2: Correcting for changes in value of investments you owned during the year** | | | |
| Net worth today | | | $______ |
| – Net worth 1 year ago | | | $______ |
| – Appreciation of investments (over past year) | | | $______ |
| + Depreciation of investments (over past year) | | | $______ |
| = Savings rate | | | $______ |

*Note:* If you save, say, $200 per month for a few months, and then you spend it all on auto repairs, you're not really saving. If you contributed $5,000 to an individual retirement account (IRA), for example, but you depleted money that you had from long ago (in other words, money that wasn't saved during the past year), don't count the $5,000 IRA contribution as new savings.

Most folks should be saving at least 5 to 10 percent of their annual income for longer-term financial goals such as retirement (Chapter 3 helps you to fine-tune your savings goals). If you're not saving that much, be sure to read the section "Tracking Expenses: From Lattes to Rent" earlier in this chapter to find out how to reduce your spending and increase your savings.

# Calculating Your Financial Net Worth

Your financial net worth is an important barometer of your monetary health. Your net worth indicates your capacity to accomplish major financial goals, such as buying a home, retiring, and withstanding unexpected expenses or loss of income.

Your *net worth* is your financial assets minus your financial liabilities:

Financial Assets – Financial Liabilities = Net Worth

The following sections explain how to determine those numbers.

## Adding up your financial assets

A *financial asset* is real money or an investment you can convert into your favorite currency that you can use to buy things now or in the future. Financial assets generally include the money you have in bank accounts, stocks, bonds, mutual funds, and exchange-traded funds (see Chapter 5, which deals with investments). Money that you have in retirement accounts (including those with your employer) and the value of any businesses or real estate that you own are also counted.

TIP

I generally recommend that you exclude your personal residence when figuring your financial assets. Include your home only if you expect to sell it someday or otherwise live off the money you now have tied up in it (perhaps by taking out a reverse mortgage). If you plan on eventually tapping into the *equity* (the difference between the market value and any debt owed on the property), add that portion of the equity that you expect to use to your list of assets.

Assets can also include your future expected Social Security benefits and pension payments (if your employer has such a plan). These assets are usually quoted in dollars per month rather than as a lump sum value. In Table 2-3, I explain how to account for these monthly benefits when tallying your financial assets.

Table 2-3 provides a place for you to figure your financial assets. Use the spaces provided or create your own spreadsheet to work from.

**TABLE 2-3 Your Financial Assets**

| Account | Value |
|---|---|
| Savings and investment accounts (including retirement accounts): | |
| Example: Bank savings account | $5,000 |
| ____________________ | $_______ |
| ____________________ | $_______ |
| ____________________ | $_______ |
| ____________________ | $_______ |
| ____________________ | $_______ |
| ____________________ | $_______ |
| Subtotal = | $_______ |
| Benefits earned that pay a monthly retirement income: | |
| Employer's pensions | $_______/month |
| Social Security | $_______/month |
| | ×240* |
| Subtotal = | $_______ |
| Total Financial Assets (add the two subtotals) = | $_______ |

***To convert benefits that will be paid to you monthly into a total dollar amount, and for purposes of simplification, assume that you will spend 20 years in retirement. Inflation may reduce the value of your employer's pension if it doesn't contain a cost-of-living increase each year in the same way that Social Security does. Don't sweat this now — you can take care of that concern in the section on retirement planning in Chapter 7.**

**REMEMBER**

Consumer items — such as your car, clothing, computer, smartphone, and so forth — do *not* count as financial assets. I understand that adding these things to your assets makes your assets *look* larger (and some financial software and publications encourage you to list these items as assets), but you can't live off them unless you sell and do without them.

## Subtracting your financial liabilities

To arrive at your financial net worth, you must subtract your *financial liabilities* from your assets. Liabilities include loans and debts outstanding, such as student loans, and credit card and auto-loan debts. When figuring your liabilities, include money you borrowed from family and friends — unless you're not expected to pay it back!

Include mortgage debt on your home as a liability *only* if you include the value of your home in your asset list. Be sure to also include debt owed on other real estate — no matter what (because you count the value of investment real estate as an asset).

## Crunching your numbers

Now comes the potentially depressing part — figuring out your debts and loans in Table 2-4.

**TABLE 2-4 Your Financial Liabilities**

| Loan | Balance |
|---|---|
| Example: Bank Credit Card | $4,000 |
| ____________________ | $______ |
| ____________________ | $______ |
| ____________________ | $______ |
| ____________________ | $______ |
| ____________________ | $______ |
| ____________________ | $______ |
| Total Financial Liabilities = | $______ |

Now you can subtract your liabilities from your assets to figure your net worth in Table 2-5.

**TABLE 2-5 Your Net Worth**

| Find | Write It Here |
|---|---|
| Total Financial Assets (from Table 2-3) | $______ |
| Total Financial Liabilities (from Table 2-4) | $______ |
| Net Worth = | $______ |

### Interpreting your net worth results

Your net worth is important and useful only to you and your unique situation and goals. What seems like a lot of money to a person with a simple lifestyle may seem like a pittance to a person with high expectations and a desire for an opulent lifestyle.

In Chapter 7, you can crunch numbers to determine your overall financial health more precisely for goals such as retirement planning. I also discuss saving toward other important goals in that chapter. In the meantime, if your net worth (excluding expected monthly retirement benefits such as those from Social Security and pensions) is negative or less than half your annual income, take notice. If you're in your 20s and you're just starting to work, a low net worth is less concerning and not unusual. Focus on turning this number positive over the next several years. However, if you're in your 30s or older, consider this a wake-up call to aggressively address your financial situation.

Getting rid of your debts — the highest-interest-rate ones first — is the most important thing. Then you want to build a safety reserve equal to three to six months of living expenses. Your overall plan should involve getting out of debt (Chapter 4), reducing your spending (see "Tracking Expenses: From Lattes to Rent" earlier in this chapter), and developing tax-wise ways to save and invest your future earnings (Chapter 9).

## Emergency Funds: Because Life Throws Curveballs

Having a plan and a strategy are all well and good, until something happens that upsets that plan. And, sooner or later, something will create some, or a lot of, havoc in your life.

Economies go through cycles. Good times and periods of growth and more jobs are inevitably followed by downturns and times (such as the COVID-19 pandemic) when more people lose their jobs or face reduced salaries.

Over the generations, there have been plenty of economic and financial crises. In addition to crises in the broader economy or society, plenty of people are hit with a personal or household-specific crisis. These can include things such as the following:

- Job loss or reduced employment income
- Medical problems
- Caring for an elderly relative
- Divorce
- Death of a spouse

## Preparing financially for the unexpected

Because you don't know what the future holds, preparing for the unexpected is financially wise. Even if you're the lucky sort who sometimes finds $5 bills on street corners, you can't control the sometimes-chaotic world in which we live.

Conventional wisdom says that you should have approximately six months' worth of living expenses put away for an emergency. This amount may or may not be right for you, because it depends, of course, on how expensive the emergency is. Why six months, anyway? And where should you put it?

TIP

How much of an emergency stash you need depends on your situation. I recommend saving the following emergency amounts under differing circumstances:

- **Three months' living expenses:** Choose this option if you have other accounts, such as a 401(k), or family members and close friends whom you can tap for a short-term loan. This minimalist approach makes sense when you're trying to maximize investments elsewhere (for example, in retirement accounts) or you have stable sources of income (employment or otherwise).
- **Six months' living expenses:** This amount is appropriate if you don't have other places to turn for a loan or you have some instability in your employment situation or source of income.
- **Up to one year's living expenses:** Set aside this much if your income fluctuates wildly from year to year or if your profession involves a high risk of job loss, finding another

job can take you a long time, and you don't have other places to turn for a loan.

TIP

If your only current source of emergency funds is a high-interest credit card, first save at least three months' worth of living expenses in an accessible account before funding a retirement account or saving for other goals.

## Assessing your resources

You've got resources — probably more than you realize. Some will be more attractive to tap than others. This section helps you recognize, inventory, and prioritize what you've got to bring to the battle.

### Tapping into accessible money and spending options

First, do an inventory of your available options for quickly (or reasonably quickly) available cash. Here are the common ones that you likely have access to and how I think about their attractiveness for you to consider tapping them:

- **Accessing your emergency reserve of cash:** I've always recommended that folks have an emergency stash of cash of at least three months' worth of living expenses, and perhaps as much as six to twelve months' worth for those with more uncertainty regarding their jobs and overall situations. Saving automatically through regular contributions to savings or transfers from checking can build your emergency fund.
- **Tapping cash value life insurance balances:** Insurance agents love to sell cash value life insurance because it pays them much higher commissions than term life insurance. If you have a cash balance in your life insurance policy, you can generally tap it by borrowing against it or by cashing in the policy. If you need life insurance, please don't do the latter until you have first secured replacement term life insurance. See Chapter 8 for more about life insurance and how to best buy it.
- **Taking out a loan.** For most people, the quickest way to borrow money (in other words, spend money you don't have) is via a credit card. If that's the only source of funding

accessible to you, be sure to shop around for a credit card with good overall terms, especially for the interest rate charged on balances carried over month-to-month. While you may be able to borrow through loans tied to other specific purchases, such as a car or furniture, when times are tough, you likely won't be in a situation where you "need" to make such purchases.

- **Borrowing from your retirement funds.** Your retirement plan may allow borrowing. I'm generally not a fan of this approach because if you borrow this money, you will miss out on the returns on that money until your loan is repaid. If the overall economy is going through a bad period, this will likely mean missing out on a good stock market rebound, since the financial markets are forward-looking and stocks rebound well in advance of the economy actually looking better. Also, if you fail to repay a loan made against your retirement account, you will get socked with federal and state income taxes on the amount withdrawn as well as federal and state tax penalties for taking a withdrawal before age 59½.

Another option you may consider is to borrow from family, and that's the subject of the next section.

## Finding assistance from family

Here are the elements or ingredients that I think generally lead to a successful lender/borrower situation between family members:

- **Borrow from someone financially sound.** The person doing the lending should be financially well off and not harmed in a notable way in the unlikely event that the borrower ends up not being able to repay part or even all of the loan.
- **Get it in writing.** The terms of the loan are put in writing and signed by both parties. One page may be sufficient in most cases. This step is critical to ensure that both parties are literally on the same page! Doing such an agreement leaves no ambiguity about the fact that both sides agree that it's a loan that needs to be repaid under the terms spelled out in the short agreement.
- **Set the loan for a reasonable (in other words, not long) period of time.** Generally speaking, the shorter the time

period for the loan, the better in terms of the loan being likely to be repaid. Of course, the repayment terms need to be realistic and fit within the budget of the borrower.

- **Charge a fair interest rate.** Loans in the real world from real-world lenders charge interest. Loans between family members can certainly be done at lower interest rates than a for-profit lender would charge.
- **Consider "what-ifs."** Your simple loan agreement should spell out things like what happens to the loan if the borrower is unable to make payments for some period of time. The loan document should also cover things like whether it's okay to pay off the loan early and what happens to the loan if something happens to the borrower.

In many cases where I have observed or heard that a family loan didn't work out or caused a rift, no loan agreement/document was in place. It's not that the document makes everything work out, but it's the process of discussing the issues and the fact that it's a loan that is expected to be repaid that helps maximize the chances that all will be good.

## Ensuring adequate insurance coverage

Carrying and maintaining catastrophic insurance is essential to protect your personal financial situation and your family. You certainly don't want to lose or misuse such coverage when you're entering or in the midst of an economic downturn or personal crisis.

Many folks have various insurance coverages (for example, health insurance and disability insurance) through their employers. You need to stay on top of securing needed insurance so that if you lose your job, you don't suffer any lapses in coverage.

WARNING

When money is tight and times are tough, you may be tempted to cut some corners and go without needed insurance for a "short time." Please don't do that! It's impossible to predict exactly when you will need to use a particular insurance policy, so you need to maintain your coverage all the time. Don't tempt fate and risk having a major insurance claim during a period when you choose to drop a particular policy in an effort to save a little money. See Chapter 8 for all the details on what insurance you should and shouldn't carry and how and where to get the best value for your insurance dollars.

## Surveying societal safety nets

The requirements or thresholds to qualify for societal safety nets vary greatly. I find that many folks are surprised at how affluent you can be and how high your income can be to qualify for some of them. The point of this section is to explain to you what's out there and get the process started for you to determine whether you may qualify for any of them.

### Health insurance subsidies

When the Affordable Care Act (ACA), also known as Obamacare, was signed into law in 2010, it included subsidies for low- and moderate-income earners. The large COVID-19 relief bill known as the American Rescue Plan Act (ARP) of 2021 further expanded and increased those subsidies to include even more households that would be considered middle class and upper-middle class. Because assets aren't an explicit factor in determining subsidies, some households that may be considered higher-income earners are also now eligible for at least partial subsidies.

Health insurance is vital insurance to continue at all times. However, as you get older and have dependents, the cost of health insurance can get quite high. Policies are also pricy due to the mandated benefits on health insurance policies under Obamacare.

Here are some other factors to consider:

- **Employer coverage:** If you work for an employer that offers health insurance coverage, you probably won't be eligible for an exchange-based plan with subsidies, but there are exceptions. Your employer should be able to supply information and data that shows whether their plan is deemed "affordable" for you and if it meets the minimum value requirement.
- **Medicare:** Medicare is the federal government–provided insurance for older Americans that kicks in for most people at age 65. If you are eligible for Medicare (and even if you're not currently enrolled in it), you may not sign up for a new Obamacare exchange-based plan. If your household contains a mix of people, some of whom are not Medicare eligible and some who are, those who are not Medicare eligible may sign up for an exchange-based and subsidized policy.

» **Medicaid:** Medicaid is a state-based health insurance program that doesn't charge premiums for low-income people. Numerous states have elected to expand their Medicaid programs so that more people are eligible for them. You can't sign up for an exchange-based subsidized health insurance plan if you're eligible for Medicaid in your state.

For more information about Medicaid, visit `www.healthcare.gov`, your state's health insurance marketplace if it has one, or your state's Medicaid program office — see the list at `www.medicaid.gov/state-overviews/index.html`.

TIP

The Kaiser Family Foundation has a super-duper useful health insurance subsidy calculator that requires your entering just a handful of inputs like your state, zip code, household income, age of family members, and so on. Once entered, the calculator (`www.kff.org/interactive/subsidy-calculator/`) will tell you approximately what coverage in the various tiers (for example, Silver and Bronze) of the health insurance plan will cost you after factoring in estimated subsidies.

The Kaiser Family Foundation's health insurance subsidy calculator also factors in how each state handles Medicaid, so by using their calculator, you will be able to estimate your potential eligibility for Medicaid.

## Unemployment insurance benefits

If you lose your job, you can probably collect unemployment insurance benefits while you're seeking a new job. Employers pay into unemployment insurance funds for this very reason — so that the government has funding to pay out benefits when folks lose their jobs.

As a point of pride or embarrassment, some folks are reluctant to even consider filing for unemployment benefits. Please don't think that way. Think of unemployment insurance as any other insurance policy you carry, such as your car policy. You hope you don't need that insurance, but if you do, you should file a claim and collect.

Being able to collect these benefits has nothing to do with your overall financial situation and neediness or lack thereof. Your spouse could still be at their well-paying job, you may have a good deal of money saved and invested, and so forth. Unemployment benefits are for those who have lost their jobs and who meet the criteria for their state to collect benefits, which have nothing to do with your current overall personal financial situation for you and yours.

The federal government, through the Department of Labor, provides federal guidelines for the state-administered unemployment benefit programs. Each state has its own eligibility guidelines for qualifying to collect unemployment benefits. These guidelines generally are based upon needing to meet a time-worked threshold or wage amount.

To find your state's unemployment information, visit `www.careeronestop.org/LocalHelp/UnemploymentBenefits/find-unemployment-benefits.aspx`.

## Federal refundable tax credits

There are two separate federal income tax credits — the Earned Income Tax Credit (EITC) and the Child Tax Credit (CTC) — which are designed to assist lower-income earners. Both of these tax credits include refundable portions, which means that even if you owe no federal income tax for a particular tax year (which is the case for more than 40 percent of all households), the federal government will actually pay you for a portion of the qualifying federal income tax credit. So, rather than owing or paying any federal income tax for that year, qualifying households are paid money by the federal government.

The EITC was instituted in 1975 and has been modified numerous times since. Eligibility for this tax credit is based upon family size and the amount of earned income. To see if you qualify for the EITC, you can answer a series of questions on the "EITC Assistant" at the IRS's website: `https://apps.irs.gov/app/eitc`.

## Help with housing

Federal Housing Assistance programs are administered by the Department of Housing and Urban Development (HUD). Their most well-known and utilized program is the Housing Choice Voucher Program, which is also known as Section 8 or the Tenant Based Rental Assistance program. It is run and administered by local Public Housing Agencies (PHAs), which distribute vouchers to help pay a portion of an eligible tenant's rent.

Eligible tenants have incomes that are below 50 percent of the median income for the county or metropolitan area in which they reside. The program ensures that a family's housing expense won't exceed 30 percent of that family's income.

Families may use the voucher for any housing that meets HUD's health and safety standards. HUD pays the voucher directly to the landlord. Tenants make their portion of the rental payment directly to their landlord as well.

For more information about this HUD program, please visit www.hud.gov/topics/housing_choice_voucher_program_section_8. Also, HUD's Resource Locator can be found at resources.hud.gov/.

## For more information on safety net programs . . .

U.C. Davis's Center for Poverty and Inequality Research has a compilation of the major federal safety net programs in the United States. Visit: poverty.ucdavis.edu/article/war-poverty-and-todays-safety-net-0.

IN THIS CHAPTER

» Stashing your cash in savings accounts

» Managing your money with software, apps, and internet resources

# Chapter 3
# Saving Like a Pro

Working toward just about any financial goal requires having a strategy in place to save money. In this chapter, I describe the benefits of different types of saving and investing accounts and help you determine which account types best meet your needs. I also provide an overview of how you can use software, apps, and internet resources to manage your finances.

## Savings Accounts 101: Where to Stash Your Cash

When income comes to you and you need to pay bills and hold onto excess savings, you'll want to have financial accounts with trustworthy and secure companies. Historically, banks have been the most often chosen institution, especially transaction (also known as checking) accounts, which are the workhorse of most people's accounts. Additional accounts for savings and investing also make sense for most people.

Here is a quick overview of your options:

- **Transaction/checking accounts:** Transaction/checking accounts are best used for depositing your monthly income and paying your bills. If you want to have unlimited bill paying and check-writing privileges and access to your money with an ATM card, checking accounts at local banks are often your best bet.
- **Savings accounts and money-market funds:** Savings accounts are available through banks; money-market funds are available through mutual-fund companies. Savings accounts and money-market funds are nearly identical, except that the best money-market funds generally pay a higher rate of interest. The interest rate paid to you, also known as the *yield,* fluctuates over time, depending on the level of interest rates in the overall economy. (Note that some banks offer money-market accounts, which are basically like savings accounts and shouldn't be confused with money-market mutual *funds.*)

  ***Note:*** The federal government backs bank savings accounts with FDIC insurance. Money-market funds are not insured. But don't give preference to a bank account just because your investment (principal) is insured. In fact, your preference should lean toward money-market funds, because the better ones are higher-yielding than the better bank savings accounts. Even though money-market funds are not insured, your investment is safe given the types of short-term, high-quality securities they invest in. And money-market funds offer check-writing and other easy ways to access your money.

  As with money you put into bank savings accounts, money-market funds are suitable for money that you can't afford to see dwindle in value.
- **Investment accounts:** Investment brokerage firms, mutual-fund companies, insurance companies, banks, and other types of financial services companies offer various types of investments. You can also invest in real estate and small, privately held companies.

  REMEMBER

  Understanding how to best invest your money given your personal and financial goals is perhaps the most important aspect of managing your money. See Chapter 5 for more information and details.

## Getting Help from Technology: Let Robots Do the Work

You can access major repositories of personal finance information through your computer. Although the lines are blurring among these categories, they're roughly defined as software, apps, and the internet:

- *Software* refers to computer programs that are available to be downloaded online. Most of the mass-marketed financial software packages sell for under $100. If you've ever used a word-processing program such as Microsoft Word or a spreadsheet program such as Microsoft Excel, then you've used software.
- *Apps,* which you download onto a smartphone or tablet, are kind of like software. They run on your phone and tend to be less costly (albeit generally less sophisticated) than computer software.
- *The internet* refers to sites that provide information and services to help you manage your financial life, including online bill paying. Most of the financial stuff on the internet is supplied by companies marketing their wares and, hence, is available for free. Some sites sell their content for a fee. (Flip to Chapter 1 for more about identifying unreliable sources of information on the internet.)

This section gives you an overview of how to use technology, software, apps, and cyberspace with your finances. (You may hear the term *fintech*, which is simply a shorthanded way of referring to financial technology or the integration of technology into companies in the financial services industry.)

### Assessing financial software

Although the number of personal-finance software packages, apps, and websites is large and growing, quality is lagging behind quantity, especially among the free internet sites. The best software programs can

- Guide you to better organization and management of your personal finances

- Help you complete mundane tasks or complex calculations quickly and easily and provide basic advice in unfamiliar territory
- Make you feel in control of your financial life

Mediocre and bad software, on the other hand, can make you feel stupid or, at the very least, make you want to scream. Lousy packages usually end up in the software graveyard.

Too many packages assume that you already know things such as your tax rate, your mortgage options, and the difference between stock and bond mutual funds. Some of what's out there is too technically oriented and isn't user-friendly, and in the worst cases, even financially flawed.

A good software package, like a good tax or financial advisor, helps you better manage your finances. It simply and concisely explains financial terminology, and it helps you make decisions by offering choices and recommendations, allowing you to "play" with alternatives before following a particular course of action. Later in this chapter, I recommend some of my favorite financial software.

## Understanding how apps can benefit and harm your bottom line

Large companies offer most apps as another option for their customers to be in touch with and interact with what they offer. The financial institutions that you do business with — banks, mutual-fund companies, brokerage firms, and so on — are common examples. Here's what to be aware of to be able to get the most out of apps without suffering harm:

- **Use apps to solve problems and perform financial tasks more efficiently.** You can use apps to do an increasing number of tasks that previously needed to be done online and through a regular computer. The dizzying pace of technological change continues as many smartphones function as minicomputers in your hand. The best apps can help you to solve common challenges such as getting better value when shopping for a specific product or service, tracking where you're spending money, checking your bank account balance, doing basic investment research, and so forth. Although some apps are provided free of charge by companies that are seeking to promote their own services, others charge modest fees (like a software company does) because the app is all they're "selling."

- **Beware the downside to "free" apps.** Although they haven't gotten the attention that computer viruses, computer malware, and computer ransomware attacks have garnered, similar problems have arisen with smartphone apps. Some will end up tracking and spying on you. The worst are scams and/or some sort of virus or malware. In addition to those issues, make sure you check out the background and agenda of any company offering a financial app and how it may be making money from the app. The worst apps are nothing more than glorified advertising from the company behind the app. Sure, they may dangle something seemingly helpful (for example, offering a free credit score, stock quotes, and so on), but be sure you uncover what their agenda and reputation ultimately are. Many free credit score apps, for example, make money from affiliate fees from credit cards they pitch you.
- **Use apps only from legitimate companies with lengthy track records.** You'll notice that most of the companies recommended in this chapter are fairly large companies with lengthy track records of success. For sure, technology is disrupting and changing many industries and companies, but that doesn't mean that you should do business only with firms that exist solely online, in the cloud, and so on. Research the history of companies with which you're considering doing business. When seeking the link for a mobile app, get that link and download the app from the company's website so you're sure you are getting the actual app rather than a knock off or a fraudulent one. Do your homework and research an app before downloading and beginning to use it. Check with more than one independent source and read independent reviews, especially those that are critical and less than flattering. And stay far away from apps that claim that they can show you how to make big bucks doing little from the comfort of your own home.
- **Consider the alternatives to an app.** Before downloading and using an app, question the need for it and consider the alternatives. Remember that the company behind the app

wants to tie you to it so you'll buy more and spend more with them. Is that your goal? You likely have your phone with you all the time. Do you really want this app running and in your face all the time? Maybe, maybe not — think about it and examine the alternatives.

## Managing your money with software and apps

Although a computer and, to a lesser extent, a smartphone may assist you with your personal finances, they simply represent a couple of many tools. Computers are best for tasks such as performing many calculations in a spreadsheet quickly and aiding you with research. Your smartphone is a good vehicle for using apps that can check on an investment balance or recent transaction.

Part of financial literacy is knowing which personal financial tasks your computer, tablet, or smartphone can best assist you with. In the following sections, I describe my favorite software, apps, and websites to help you accomplish these chores.

### Tracking your money

Apps can come in handy for tracking your money. Check out the following apps:

- **Goodbudget:** This app is great for its simplicity and practicality. The basic version provides you with up to one year of expense-tracking history in ten main categories (envelopes). A paid or premium version ($70 per year) that provides up to seven years of expense tracking with unlimited categories as well as email support is also available. I suggest starting with the free version and then deciding in the future whether an upgrade is worth your while.
- **GasBuddy:** Some apps are simply designed to save you money. GasBuddy, for example, shows you the price for gasoline at various service stations in a local area. It's free for consumers to use.
- **Tollsmart:** Especially when going on lengthy car trips, car tolls can add up quickly. This low-cost app enables you to compare toll costs for alternative routes.

- **CamelCamelCamel:** This app is a price tracker that scans items on Amazon, shows you their price history, and sends you alerts when a product you're interested in drops in price. (**PriceGrabber** scans items everywhere online, although its website is much easier to use than its app.)

TIP

Quicken is a good software program that helps with expense tracking and bill paying. In addition to offering check paying and electronic bill-payment, Quicken is a financial organizer. The program allows you to list your investments and other assets, along with your loans and other financial liabilities. Quicken automates the process of paying your bills, and it can track your check-writing and prepare reports that detail your spending by category so you can find the fat in your budget. (For a complete discussion on how to track your spending, see Chapter 2.)

TIP

You can avoid dealing with paper checks — written or printed — by signing up for online bill payment. With such services, you save on checks, stamps, and envelopes. These services are available to anyone with a checking account through many banks, credit unions, and brokerage firms, as well as through Quicken.

## Planning for retirement

Good retirement-planning tools can help you plan for retirement by crunching the numbers for you. They can also teach you how particular changes — such as your investment returns, the rate of inflation, or your savings rate — can affect when and in what style you can retire. The biggest time-saving aspect of retirement-planning tools is that they let you more quickly play with and see the consequences of changing the assumptions.

Here are two major investment companies to consider that provide high-quality, low-cost retirement-planning tools:

- **T. Rowe Price's website** (`www.troweprice.com`) has several tools, including its "Retirement Income Calculator," (`www.troweprice.com/usis/advice/tools/retirement-income-calculator`) that can help you determine where you stand in terms of reaching a given retirement goal. Expect some marketing of T. Rowe Price's mutual funds with its tools.

- **Vanguard's website** (www.vanguard.com) can help with figuring savings goals to reach retirement goals as well as with managing your budget and assets in retirement. See their tools and calculators at investor.vanguard.com/tools-calculators/overview.

## Preparing your taxes

Good, properly used tax-preparation software can save you time and money. The best programs "interview" you to gather the necessary information and select the appropriate forms based on your responses. Of course, you're still the one responsible for locating all the information needed to complete your return. More-experienced taxpayers can bypass the interview and jump directly to the forms they know they need to complete. These programs also help flag overlooked deductions and identify other tax-reducing strategies.

TurboTax, H&R Block Tax Software, TaxAct, and Tax Slayer are the leading tax-preparation programs.

In addition to the federal tax packages, tax-preparation programs are available for state income taxes, too. Many state tax forms are fairly easy to complete because they're based on information from your federal form. If your state tax forms are based on your federal form and simple, you may want to skip buying the state income-tax preparation packages and prepare your state return by hand.

TIP

If you're mainly looking for federal income tax forms, you can get them at no charge through the IRS's website (www.irs.gov).

## Researching investments

Gone are the days of schlepping off to the library to look at investing reference manuals, buying print versions for your own use, or slogging through voice-mail hell when you call government agencies. Today you can access these and other investing resources on your computer. You can also often pay for just what you need:

- **The SEC:** The Securities and Exchange Commission (SEC) allows unlimited, free access to its documents at www.sec.gov. All public corporations, as well as mutual funds, file their reports with the agency. Be aware, however, that navigating this site takes some patience.

- **Morningstar:** You can access Morningstar's individual stock and mutual-fund reports at www.morningstar.com. The basic reports are free, but they're watered-down versions of the company's comprehensive software and paper products. If you want to buy Morningstar's unabridged fund reports online, you can do so for a fee.
- **Vanguard:** Although I'm leery of financial service company "educational" materials because of bias and self-serving advice, some companies do a worthy job on these materials. The investor-friendly, thrifty Vanguard Group of mutual funds and ETFs has an app and website (www.vanguard.com), where investors can learn the basics of fund investing. Additionally, investors in Vanguard's funds can access up-to-date personal account information through the site.

### Accessing economic and financial data

The St. Louis Fed's Federal Reserve Economic Database — also known as FRED — is accessible online at fred.stlouisfed.org and through an app. Here's a rare case where you can have a wealth of data on the economy and financial markets at your fingertips and never be bombarded with ads or plugs to buy things.

### Trading online

If you do your investing homework, trading securities online may save you money and perhaps some time. For years, discount brokers were heralded as the low-cost source for trading.

TIP

A number of major brokerage firms have eliminated online trading fees on stock and exchange-traded funds. Quality firms offering "free" brokerage trades on stocks and ETFs include Charles Schwab, E-Trade, Fidelity, Interactive Brokers, T. Rowe Price, and Vanguard. These changes have reduced the attractiveness of online-only trading firms like Robinhood given the other high fees and sub-par terms offered on their accounts, services, and investments to make up for their free brokerage trades. Investors should always consider and evaluate the entire package of services when deciding on an investment firm through which to do business.

By eliminating the overhead of branch offices and by accepting and processing trades online, these online-only brokers keep their costs and brokerage charges to a minimum. However, some of these brokers have limited products and services. For example, some don't offer many of the best mutual funds. And my own experience with reaching live people at some online brokers has been trying — I've had to wait on hold for more than ten minutes before a customer service representative answered the call.

REMEMBER

Although online trading may save you on transaction costs, it can also encourage you to trade more than you should, resulting in higher total trading costs, lower investment returns, and higher income-tax bills. Following investments on a daily basis encourages you to think short term. Remember that the best investments are bought and held for the long haul (see Chapter 5 for more information).

## Reading and searching periodicals

Many business and financial publications are online, offering investors news and financial market data. The *Wall Street Journal* provides an online, personalized edition of the paper (www.wsj.com) that allows you to tailor the content to meet your specific needs. The price, currently discounted, is $104 for a 12-month subscription.

Leading business publications such as *Forbes* (www.forbes.com) and *Businessweek* (www.bloomberg.com/businessweek) put their current magazines' content on the internet. Some publications are charging for archived articles and for some current content for nonsubscribers to their print magazine.

WARNING

Be careful to take what you read and hear in the mass media with many grains of salt. Much of the content revolves around tweaking people's anxieties and dwelling on the latest crises and fads.

My website (www.erictyson.com) includes analysis of current news and highlights and summarizes the best content from many sources and sites, including leading newsletters.

## Automating investment services

Numerous websites offer an automated investing service. These sites purport to help you choose an overall investment mix (asset allocation) and then divvy that money up, typically among exchange-traded funds. Over time, the allocations can be tweaked or adjusted based on some predetermined formulas.

For this largely automated service, so-called robo advisors like Betterment and WealthFront generally charge around 0.25 percent to 0.5 percent per year of the assets they are managing. I believe that you can educate yourself enough about investing in funds that paying an ongoing fee for such services isn't worth it. (If you're really interested in such services, Vanguard Digital Advisor has low fees and minimums.)

## Buying life insurance

If loved ones are financially dependent on you, you probably know you need life insurance. But add together the dread of life-insurance salespeople and a fear of death, and you have a recipe for procrastination. Although your computer can't stave off the Grim Reaper, it can help you find a quality, low-cost policy that can be more than 80 percent less costly than the most expensive options, all without having you deal with high-pressure sales tactics.

The best way to shop for term life insurance online is through one of the quotation services I discuss in Chapter 8. At each of these sites, you fill in your date of birth, whether you smoke, how much coverage you'd like, and for how long you'd like to lock in the initial premium. When you're done filling in this information, a new web page pops up with a list of low-cost quotes (based on assumed good health) from highly rated (for financial stability) insurance companies.

## Preparing legal documents

Just as you can prepare a tax return with good software, you can also prepare common legal documents. This type of software may save you from the often-difficult task of finding a competent and affordable attorney.

Using legal software is generally preferable to using fill-in-the-blank documents. Software has the built-in virtues of directing and limiting your choices and preventing you from making common mistakes. Quality software also incorporates the knowledge and insights of the legal eagles who developed the software. And it can save you money.

If your situation isn't unusual, legal software may work well for you. As to the legality of documents that you create with legal software, remember that a will, for example, is made legal and valid by your witnesses; the fact that an attorney prepares the document is *not* what makes it legal.

TIP

An excellent package for preparing your own will is Quicken WillMaker Plus, which is published by Nolo Press, a name synonymous with high quality and user-friendliness in the legal publishing world. In addition to allowing you to prepare wills, WillMaker can also help you prepare a living will and medical power of attorney document. The software also allows you to create a living trust that serves to keep property out of probate in the event of your death. Like wills, living trusts are fairly standard legal documents that you can properly create with the guidance of a top-notch software package. The package advises you to seek professional guidance for your situation, if necessary. If you establish a login on their website at `www.nolo.com/`, discounts of 25 to 30 percent on Quicken WillMaker Plus during special holidays will be sent to your email. On Black Friday, Cyber Monday, and in December, the discount is 50 percent.

IN THIS CHAPTER

» Distinguishing between good debt and bad debt

» Managing good, bad, and unexpected debt

» Repaying debt

» Stopping the spending/consumer debt cycle

# Chapter 4
# Debt Demystified

Debt can be an emotional topic for most people. Some carry balances on their credit cards or may struggle to afford college. Unanticipated events in the absence of a sufficient emergency fund can pile on surprise debt (and stress).

This chapter helps you recognize the difference between good debt and bad debt. I show how to plan and use debt to your financial advantage and share strategies for paying off debt and stopping the spending/consumer debt cycle.

## Good Debt versus Bad Debt

Why do you borrow money? Usually, you borrow money because you don't have enough to buy something you want or need — like a college education. A four-year college education can easily cost $100,000, $150,000, $200,000, $250,000, or more. Most people don't have that kind of spare cash. So borrowing money to finance part of that cost enables you to buy the education.

How about a new car? A trip to your friendly local car dealer shows you that a new set of wheels will set you back $25,000+. Although more people may have the money to pay for that than, say, the college education, what if you don't? Should you finance the car the way you finance the education?

There's a *big* difference between borrowing for something that represents a long-term investment and borrowing for short-term consumption. I'm not saying that you shouldn't buy a car. The point is to *spend what you can afford.* If you have to borrow money in the form of an outstanding balance on your credit card for many months in order to buy a car (or take the vacation, or whatever), then you *can't afford* it.

## Consuming your way to bad debt

I coined the term *bad debt* to refer to debt incurred for consumption, because such debt is harmful to your long-term financial health.

You'll be able to take many more vacations during your lifetime if you save the cash in advance. If you get into the habit of borrowing and paying all the associated interest for vacations, cars, clothing, and other consumer items, you'll spend more of your future income paying back the debt and interest, leaving you with less money for your other goals.

The relatively high interest rates that banks and other lenders charge for bad (consumer) debt is one of the reasons you're less able to save money when using such debt. Not only does money borrowed through credit cards, auto loans, and other types of consumer loans carry a relatively high interest rate, but it also isn't tax-deductible.

TIP

I'm not saying that you should never borrow money and that all debt is bad. Good debt, such as that used to buy real estate and small businesses, is generally available at lower interest rates than bad debt and is usually tax-deductible. If well managed, these investments may also increase in value. Borrowing to pay for educational expenses can also make sense. Education is generally a good long-term investment because it can increase your earning potential. And student loan interest is tax-deductible, subject to certain limitations. Taking out good debt, however, should be done in proper moderation and for acquiring quality assets. See the section later in this chapter, "Assessing good debt: Can you get too much?"

## Recognizing bad debt overload

Calculating how much debt you have relative to your annual income is a useful way to size up your debt load. Ignore, for now, good debt — the loans you may owe on real estate, a business, an education, and so on (I get to that in the next section). I'm focusing on bad debt, the higher-interest debt used to buy items that depreciate in value.

To calculate your bad debt danger ratio, divide your bad debt by your annual income. For example, suppose you earn $40,000 per year. Between your credit cards and an auto loan, you have $20,000 of debt. In this case, your bad debt represents 50 percent of your annual income.

$$\frac{\text{bad debt}}{\text{annual income}} = \text{bad debt danger ratio}$$

REMEMBER

*The financially healthy amount of bad debt is zero.* While enjoying the convenience of credit cards, *never* buy anything with your credit card(s) that you can't afford to pay off in full when the bill comes at the end of the month. Not everyone agrees with me. One major U.S. credit card company says — in its "educational" materials, which it "donates" to schools to teach students about supposedly sound financial management — that carrying consumer debt amounting to 10 to 20 percent of your annual income is just fine.

WARNING

When your bad debt danger ratio starts to push beyond 25 percent, it can spell real trouble. Such high levels of high-interest consumer debt on credit cards and auto loans grow like cancer. The growth of the debt can snowball and get out of control unless something significant intervenes. If you have consumer debt beyond 25 percent of your annual income, see the section "Strategies for Debt Repayment" later in this chapter to find out how to get out of debt.

How much good debt is acceptable? The answer varies. The key question is this: Are you able to save sufficiently to accomplish your goals? In Chapter 2, I help you figure out how much you're actually saving, and in Chapter 7, I help you determine how much you need to save to accomplish your goals. (See Chapter 7 to find out how much mortgage debt is appropriate to take on when buying a home.)

REMEMBER

Borrow money only for investments (good debt) — for purchasing things that retain and hopefully increase in value over the long term, such as an education, real estate, or your own business. Don't borrow money for consumption (bad debt) — for spending on things that decrease in value and eventually become financially worthless, such as cars, clothing, vacations, and so on.

### Assessing good debt: Can you get too much?

As with good food, you can get too much of a good thing, including good debt! When you incur debt for investment purposes — to buy real estate, for small business, even your education — you hope to see a positive return on your invested dollars.

But some real-estate investments don't work out. Some small businesses crash and burn, and some educational degrees and programs don't help in the way that students hope they will.

There's no magic formula for determining when you have too much "good debt." In extreme cases, I've seen entrepreneurs, for example, borrow up to their eyeballs to get a business off the ground. Sometimes this works, and they end up financially rewarded, but in most cases, extreme borrowing doesn't pan out.

Here are three important questions to ponder and discuss with your loved ones about the seemingly "good debt" you're taking on:

- Are you and your loved ones able to sleep well at night and function well during the day, free from great worry about how you're going to meet next month's expenses?
- Are the likely rewards worth the risk that the borrowing entails?
- Are you and your loved ones financially able to save what you'd like to work toward your goals (see Chapter 3)?

If you answer "no" to these questions, see the debt-reduction strategies in the section "Strategies for Debt Repayment" later in this chapter for more information.

## Managing Debt: Good, Bad, and Unexpected

Accumulating *bad debt* (consumer debt) by buying things like new living room furniture or a new car that you really can't afford is like living on a diet of sugar and caffeine: a quick fix with little nutritional value. Borrowing on your credit card to afford an extravagant vacation is detrimental to your long-term financial health.

When you use debt for investing in your future, I call it *good debt.* Borrowing money to pay for a quality education that improves your career, to buy real estate, or to invest in a small business is like eating a well-balanced and healthy diet. That's not to say that you can't get yourself into trouble when using good debt. Just as you can gorge yourself on too much good food, you can develop financial indigestion from too much good debt or when using debt to finance poor investments or educational options.

This section shows the planning required to manage each type of debt, including unexpected medical expenses.

## Planning for educational expenses

College can cost a lot. The total costs — including tuition, fees, books, supplies, room, board, and transportation — vary substantially from school to school. The total average annual cost is running around $59,000 per year at private colleges and around $29,000 at public colleges and universities (at the in-state rate). The more expensive schools can cost up to about one-third more. Ouch!

TIP

As with any other product or service purchase, it pays to shop around. You can find good values — colleges that offer competitive pricing *and* provide a quality education. Although you don't want to choose a college simply because it costs less, you also shouldn't make or allow a college choice without any consideration of cost.

If you are a parent and have money left over *after* taking advantage of retirement accounts, by all means, try to save for your children's college costs. You should save in your name unless you know you aren't going to apply for financial aid, including those loans that are available regardless of your economic situation.

If you're not a high-income earner, consider trying to save enough to pay a third or, at most, half of the cost. You can make up the balance through loans, your child's employment before and during college, and the like.

In Chapter 7, I describe the savings strategies that financially literate people use to prepare for college expenses.

## Using credit cards strategically

Given what I have to say about the vagaries of consumer debt, you may think that I'm always against using credit cards. Actually, I have credit cards, and I use them — but I pay my balance in full each month. Besides the convenience credit cards offer me — in not having to carry around other forms of payment such as extra cash and checks — I receive another benefit: I have free use of the bank's money until the time the bill is due. (Some cards offer other benefits, such as frequent flyer miles or other rewards, and I have those types of cards, too.) Also, purchases made on credit cards may be contested if the sellers of products or services don't stand behind what they sell.

When you charge on a credit card that *does not* have an outstanding balance carried over from the prior month, you typically have several weeks (known as the *grace period*) from the date of the charge to the time when you must pay your bill. This is called *playing the float*. Had you paid for this purchase by cash or check, you would have had to shell out your money sooner.

WARNING

If you have difficulty saving money and plastic tends to break your budget, forget the float and reward games. You're better off not using credit cards. The same applies to those who pay their bills in full but spend more because it's so easy to do with a piece of plastic.

## Anticipating medical bills

Many folks believe that most medical expenses in retirement will be covered by insurance or the government. Some think their employers will continue some version of their medical insurance coverage into retirement. Others believe Medicare covers everything for beneficiaries or is similar to the employer coverage they're used to.

Don't fall into this trap and make this mistake. In retirement, you're on your own for a great deal of your medical expenses and for long-term care. A reasonable estimate of your different health expenditures and how they'll be paid or insured needs to be part of your retirement plan.

WARNING

Fewer and fewer employers offer any medical expense insurance or coverage for their retirees. Generally, only large employers, especially those whose employees are unionized, offer retiree medical coverage. Those employers that do offer medical plans to their retirees have steadily reduced the coverage over the years. Almost all retiree medical plans reserve the right to change the terms at any time, no matter how long a beneficiary has been retired.

Chapter 2 covers setting up emergency funds for life's curveballs, which can include unplanned medical expenses (at any age). For more information about health insurance during your senior years, flip to Chapter 8.

# Strategies for Debt Repayment

Getting rid of your bad debts may be even more difficult than giving up the junk foods you love. But in the long run, you'll be glad you did; you'll be financially healthier and emotionally happier. And after you get rid of your high-cost consumer debts, make sure you practice the best way to avoid future credit problems: *Don't borrow with bad debt.*

Before you decide which debt reduction strategies make sense for you, you must first consider your overall financial situation (see Chapter 2) and assess your alternatives. (I also discuss strategies for reducing your current spending — which help you free up more cash to pay down your debts — in Chapter 2.)

## Using savings to reduce your consumer debt

Many people build a mental wall between their savings and investment accounts and their consumer debt accounts. By failing to view their finances holistically, they simply fall into the habit of looking at these accounts individually. The thought of putting a door in that big wall doesn't occur to them. This section helps you see how your savings can be used to lower your consumer debt.

### Understanding how you gain

If you have the savings to pay off consumer debt, like high-interest credit card and auto loans, consider doing so. (Make sure you pay off the loans with the highest interest rates first.)

Sure, you diminish your savings, but you also reduce your debts. Although your savings and investments may be earning decent returns, the interest you're paying on your consumer debts is likely higher.

REMEMBER

Paying off consumer loans on a credit card at, say, 12 percent is like finding an investment with a guaranteed return of 12 percent — *tax-free*. You would actually need to find an investment that yielded even more — around 18 percent — to net 12 percent after paying taxes on those investment returns in order to justify not paying off your 12 percent loans. The higher your tax bracket (see Chapter 9), the higher the return you need on your investments to justify keeping high-interest consumer debt.

Even if you think that you're an investing genius and you can earn more on your investments, swallow your ego and pay down your consumer debts anyway. In order to chase that higher potential return from investments, you need to take substantial risk. You *may* earn more investing in that hot stock tip or bargain real estate, but you probably won't.

WARNING

If you use your savings to pay down consumer debts, be careful to leave yourself enough of an emergency cushion. (In Chapter 2, I tell you how to determine what size emergency reserve you should have.) You want to be in a position to withstand an unexpected large expense or temporary loss of income. On the other hand, if you use savings to pay down credit card debt, you can run your credit card balances back up in a financial pinch (unless your card gets canceled), or you can turn to a family member or wealthy friend for a low-interest loan.

## Finding the funds to pay down consumer debts

Have you ever reached into the pocket of an old jacket and found a folded $20 bill you forgot you had? Stumbling across some forgotten funds is always a pleasant experience. But before you root through all your closets in search of stray cash to help you pay down that nagging consumer debt, check out some of these financial jacket pockets you may have overlooked:

- **Borrow against your cash value life insurance policy.** If you did business with a life insurance agent, that person probably sold you a cash value policy because it pays high commissions to insurance agents. Or perhaps your parents bought one of these policies for you when you were a child. Borrow against the cash value to pay down your debts. (***Note:*** You may want to consider discontinuing your cash value policy altogether and simply withdraw the cash.)

- **Sell investments held outside of retirement accounts.** Maybe you have some shares of stock or a Treasury bond. Consider cashing in these investments to pay down your consumer loans. Just be sure to consider the tax consequences of selling these investments. If possible, sell investments that won't generate a big tax bill.
- **Tap the equity in your home.** If you're a homeowner, you may be able to tap in to your home's *equity,* which is the difference between the property's market value and the outstanding loan balance. You can generally borrow against real estate at a lower interest rate and get a tax deduction, subject to interest deduction limitations. However, you must take care to ensure that you don't overborrow on your home and risk losing it to foreclosure.
- **Borrow against your employer's retirement account.** Check with your employer's benefits department to see whether you can borrow against your retirement account balance. The interest rate is usually reasonable. Be careful, though — if you leave or lose your job, you have to fully repay the loan by the federal income tax return due date of the following year; otherwise, the unpaid balance is treated as a taxable distribution. Also recognize that you'll miss out on investment returns on the money borrowed.
- **Lean on family.** They know you, love you, realize your shortcomings, and probably won't be as cold-hearted as some bankers. Money borrowed from family members can have strings attached, of course. Treating the obligation seriously is important. To avoid misunderstandings, write up a simple agreement listing the terms and conditions of the loan. Unless your family members are the worst bankers I know, you'll probably get a fair interest rate, and your family will have the satisfaction of helping you out. Just be sure to pay them back.

## Decreasing debt when you lack savings

If you lack savings to throw at your consumer debts, and you're currently spending all your income (and more!), you need to figure out how you can decrease your spending (see Chapter 2 for lots of great ideas) and/or increase your income. In the meantime, you need to slow the growth of your debt.

## Reducing your credit card's interest rate

Different credit cards charge different interest rates. So why pay 14, 16, or 18 percent (or more) when you can pay less? The credit card business is competitive. Until you get your debt paid off, slow the growth of your debt by reducing the interest rate you're paying. Here are sound ways to do that:

- **Apply for a lower-rate credit card.** If you're earning a decent income, you're not too burdened with debt, and you have a clean credit record, qualifying for lower-rate cards is relatively painless. Some persistence (and cleanup work) may be required if you have income and debt problems or nicks in your credit report. After you're approved for a new, lower-interest-rate card, you can simply transfer your outstanding balance from your higher-rate card.

  `CreditCards.com`'s website (`www.creditcards.com`) carries information on low-interest-rate and no-annual-fee cards (among others, including secured cards).
- **Call the bank(s) that issued your current high-interest-rate credit card(s) and say that you want to cancel your card(s) because you found a competitor that offers no annual fee and a lower interest rate.** Your bank may choose to match the terms of the "competitor" rather than lose you as a customer. Sticking with your current card may be better for you because canceling the credit card, especially if it's one you've had for a number of years, may lower your credit score in the short term.
- **While you're paying down your credit card balance(s), stop making new charges on cards that have outstanding balances.** Many people don't realize that interest starts to accumulate *immediately* when they carry a balance. *You have no grace period* — the 20 or so days you normally have to pay your balance in full without incurring interest charges — if you carry a credit card balance from month to month.

### Understanding all credit card terms and conditions

WARNING

Avoid getting lured into applying for a credit card that hypes an extremely low interest rate. One such card advertised a 1.9 percent rate, but you had to dig into the fine print for the rest of the story.

First, any card that offers such a low interest rate will honor that rate only for a short period of time — in this case, six months. After six months, the interest rate skyrocketed to nearly 15 percent.

But wait, there's more: Make just one late payment or exceed your credit limit, and the company raises your interest rate to 19.8 percent (or even 24 percent, 29 percent, or more) and slaps you with a $25 fee — $35 thereafter. If you want a cash advance on your card, you get socked with a fee equal to 3 percent of the amount advanced. (Some banks have even advertised 0 percent interest rates — although that rate generally has applied only to balances transferred from another card, and such cards have been subject to all the other vagaries discussed in this section.)

I'm not saying that everyone should avoid this type of card. Such a card may make sense for you if you want to transfer an outstanding balance and then pay off that balance within a matter of months and cancel the card to avoid getting socked with the card's high fees.

REMEMBER

If you hunt around for a low-interest-rate credit card, be sure to review all the terms and conditions. Start by reading the uniform rates and terms disclosure, which details the myriad fees and conditions (especially how much your interest rate can increase for missed or late payments). Also, be sure you understand how the future interest rate is determined on cards that charge variable interest rates.

### Cutting up your credit cards

TIP

If you have a tendency to live beyond your means by buying on credit, get rid of the culprit — the credit card (and other consumer credit). To kick the habit, a smoker needs to toss *all* the cigarettes, and an alcoholic needs to get rid of *all* the booze. Cut up *all* of your credit cards and call the card issuers to cancel your accounts. And when you buy consumer items such as cars and furniture, do not apply for the E-Z credit.

The world worked fine back in the years B.C. (Before Credit). Think about it: Just a few generations ago, credit cards didn't even exist. People paid with cash and checks — imagine that! You *can* function without buying anything on credit. In certain cases, you may need a card as collateral — such as when renting a car. When you bring back the rental car, however, you can pay with cash or a check. Leave the card at home in the back of your sock drawer or freezer, and pull (or thaw) it out only for the occasional car rental.

With the trend toward a cashless society, it may be difficult to go cash/check only, but it can be done, and getting out of debt may be an important enough reason to do so. Some businesses are saying no to cash. You could carry a charge card like the American Express, which must be paid in full each month as no credit is extended.

If you can trust yourself, keep a separate credit card *only* for new purchases that you know you can absolutely pay in full each month. No one needs three, five, or ten credit cards! You can live with one (and actually none), given the wide acceptance of most cards.

Retailers such as department stores and gas stations just love to issue cards. Not only do these cards charge outrageously high interest rates, but they're also not widely accepted like Visa and Mastercard. Virtually all retailers accept Visa and Mastercard. More credit lines mean more temptation to spend what you can't afford.

If you decide to keep one widely accepted credit card instead of getting rid of them all, be careful. You may be tempted to let debt accumulate and roll over for a month or two, starting up the whole horrible process of running up your consumer debt again. Rather than keeping one credit card, consider getting a debit card.

### Discovering debit cards: The best of both worlds?

Credit cards are the main reason today's consumers are buying more than they can afford. So logic says that one way you can keep your spending in check is to stop using your credit cards. But in a society that's used to the widely accepted Visa and Mastercard plastic for purchases, changing habits is hard. And you may be legitimately concerned that carrying your checkbook or cash can be a hassle or can be costly if you're mugged.

Debit cards potentially offer the best of both worlds. The beauty of the debit card is that it offers you the convenience of making purchases with a piece of plastic without the temptation or ability to run up credit card debt. Debit cards keep you from spending money you don't have and help you live within your means.

A *debit card* looks just like a credit card with either the Visa or Mastercard logo. The big difference between debit cards and credit cards is that, as with checks, debit-card purchase amounts are deducted electronically from your checking account within days. (Bank ATM cards are also debit cards; however, if they lack a Visa or Mastercard logo, they're accepted by far fewer merchants.)

WARNING

If you switch to a debit card and you keep your checking account balance low and don't ordinarily balance your checkbook, you may need to start balancing it. Otherwise, you may face charges for overdrawing your account.

Here are some other differences between debit and credit cards:

- If you pay your credit card bill in full and on time each month, your credit card gives you free use of the money you owe until it's time to pay the bill. Debit cards take the money out of your checking account almost immediately.
- Credit cards make it easier for you to dispute charges for problematic merchandise through the issuing bank. Most banks allow you to dispute charges for up to 60 days after purchase and will credit the disputed amount to your account pending resolution. Most debit cards offer a much shorter window, typically less than one week, for making disputes.

Because moving your checking account can be a hassle, see whether your current bank offers Visa or Mastercard debit cards. If your bank doesn't offer one, shop among the major banks in your area, which are likely to offer the cards. Because such cards come with checking accounts, make sure you do some comparison shopping among the different account features and fees.

TIP

A number of investment firms offer Visa or Mastercard debit cards with their asset management accounts. Not only can these investment firm "checking accounts" help you break the credit card overspending habit, but they may also get you thinking about saving and investing your money. One drawback of these accounts is that some of them require higher minimum initial investment amounts. Among brokerages offering accounts with debit cards and competitive investment offerings and prices are Fidelity (phone 800-343-3548; website www.fidelity.com), and Schwab (phone 800-435-4000; website www.schwab.com).

## Turning to credit counseling agencies

Prior to the passage of the 2005 bankruptcy laws that I discuss later in this chapter, each year hundreds of thousands of debt-burdened consumers sought "counseling" from credit counseling service offices. Now, more than a million people annually get the required counseling. Unfortunately, some people find that the service doesn't always work the way it's pitched.

### Beware biased advice at credit counseling agencies

Although credit counseling agencies' promotional materials and counselors aren't shy about highlighting the drawbacks to bankruptcy, counselors are reluctant to discuss the negative impact of signing up for a debt payment plan. Restructuring your credit card payments tarnishes your credit reports and scores. Counselors often neglect to mention this important fact.

TIP

Interview any counseling agency you may be considering working with. You're the customer and you should do your homework first and be in control. Don't allow anyone or any agency to make you feel that they're in a position of power simply because of your financial troubles.

### Ask questions and avoid debt management programs

Probably the most important question to ask a counseling agency is whether it offers *debt management programs* (DMPs), whereby you're put on a repayment plan with your creditors and the agency gets a monthly fee for handling the payments. You do *not* want to work with an agency offering DMPs because of conflicts of interest. An agency can't offer objective advice about all your options for dealing with debt, including bankruptcy, if it has a financial incentive to put you on a DMP.

TIP

The Institute for Financial Literacy is a good agency that doesn't offer DMPs (phone 207-873-0068; website www.financiallit.org).

Here are some additional questions that the Federal Trade Commission suggests you ask prospective counseling agencies you may hire:

- **What are your fees? Are there setup and/or monthly fees?** Get a specific price quote in writing.
- **What if I can't afford to pay your fees or make contributions?** If an organization won't help you because you can't afford to pay, look elsewhere for help.
- **Will I have a formal written agreement or contract with you?** Don't sign anything without reading it first. Make sure that all verbal promises are in writing.
- **Are you licensed to offer your services in my state?** You should work only with a licensed agency.
- **What are the qualifications of your counselors? Are they accredited or certified by an outside organization?** If so, by whom? If not, how are they trained? Try to use an organization whose counselors are trained by a non-affiliated party.
- **What assurance do I have that information about me (including my address, phone number, and financial information) will be kept confidential and secure?** A reputable agency can provide you with a clearly written privacy policy.
- **How are your employees compensated? Are they paid more if I sign up for certain services, if I pay a fee, or if I make a contribution to your organization?** Employees who work on an incentive basis are less likely to have your best interests in mind than those who earn a straight salary that isn't influenced by your choices.

## Filing bankruptcy

For consumers in over their heads, the realization that their monthly income is increasingly exceeded by their bill payments is usually a traumatic one. In many cases, years can pass before people consider a drastic measure like filing bankruptcy. Both financial and emotional issues come into play in one of the most difficult and painful, yet potentially beneficial, decisions.

## Understanding bankruptcy benefits

Bankruptcy allows certain types of debts to be completely eliminated or *discharged.* Debts that typically can be discharged include credit card, medical, auto, utilities, and rent.

Debts that may *not* be canceled generally include child support, alimony, student loans, taxes, and court-ordered damages (for example, drunk driving settlements). Ideal candidates for bankruptcy have debts (such as credit cards) that are dischargeable and a high level of high-interest consumer debt relative to their annual income. When this ratio exceeds 25 percent, filing bankruptcy may be your best option.

REMEMBER

Eliminating your debt allows you to start working toward your financial goals. Depending on the amount of debt you have outstanding relative to your income, you may need a decade or more to pay it all off. Filing bankruptcy can also offer emotional benefits by easing the constant worry caused by carrying too much debt.

## Coming to terms with bankruptcy drawbacks

Filing bankruptcy, needless to say, has a number of drawbacks. First, bankruptcy appears on your credit report for up to ten years, so you'll have difficulty obtaining credit, especially in the years immediately following your filing. However, if you already have problems on your credit report (because of late payments or a failure to pay previous debts), damage has already been done. And without savings, you're probably not going to be making major purchases (such as a home) in the next several years anyway.

REMEMBER

If you do file bankruptcy, getting credit in the future is still possible. You may be able to obtain a *secured credit card,* which requires you to deposit money in a bank account equal to the credit limit on your credit card. Of course, you'll be better off without the temptation of any credit cards and better served with a debit card. Also, know that if you can hold down a stable job, most creditors will be willing to give you loans within a few years of your filing bankruptcy. Almost all lenders ignore bankruptcy after five to seven years.

Another drawback of bankruptcy is that it costs money, and those expenses have jumped higher due to the requirements of bankruptcy laws (more on that in a moment). I know this expense seems terribly unfair. You're already in financial trouble — that's why you're filing bankruptcy! Court filing and legal fees can easily exceed $1,500, especially in higher cost-of-living areas.

And finally, most people find that filing bankruptcy causes emotional stress. Admitting that your personal income can't keep pace with your debt obligations is painful. Although filing bankruptcy clears the decks of debt and gives you a fresh financial start, feeling a profound sense of failure (and sometimes shame) is common. Bankruptcy filers are reluctant to talk about it with others, including family and friends.

Another part of the emotional side of filing bankruptcy is that you must open your personal financial affairs to court scrutiny and court control during the several months it takes to administer a bankruptcy. A court-appointed bankruptcy trustee oversees your case and tries to recover as much of your property as possible to satisfy the *creditors* — those to whom you owe money.

If you file for bankruptcy, don't feel bad about not paying back the bank. Credit cards are one of the most profitable lines of business for banks. (Now you know why your mailbox and email inbox are always stuffed with solicitations for more cards.) The nice merchants from whom you bought the merchandise have already been paid. *Charge-offs* — the banker's term for taking the loss on debt that you discharge through bankruptcy — are the banker's cost, which is another reason why the interest rate is so high on credit cards and why borrowing on them is a bad idea.

## Deciphering the bankruptcy laws

The Bankruptcy Abuse and Prevention Act of 2005 has a significant effect on consumers who are considering filing for bankruptcy. As you may be able to tell from the bill's name, major creditors, such as credit card companies, lobbied heavily for new laws. Although they didn't get everything they wanted, they got a lot, which — not surprisingly — doesn't benefit those folks in dire financial condition contemplating bankruptcy. Don't despair, though; help and information can overcome the worst provisions of this law. Here are the major elements of the personal bankruptcy laws:

- **Required counseling:** Before filing for bankruptcy, individuals must complete credit counseling, the purpose of which is to explore your options for dealing with debt, including (but not limited to) bankruptcy and developing a debt repayment plan.

  WARNING

  Historically, many supposed "counseling" agencies have provided highly biased advice. Be sure to read the earlier section "Turning to Credit Counseling Agencies" to find out what conflicts of interest agencies have and to get advice on how to pick a top-notch agency.

  To have debts discharged through bankruptcy, the new law requires a second type of counseling called "Debtor Education." All credit counseling and debtor education must be completed by an approved organization on the U.S. Trustee's website (`www.justice.gov/ust`). Click on the link Credit Counseling & Debtor Education (`www.justice.gov/ust/credit-counseling-debtor-education-information`).
- **Means testing:** Some high-income earners may be precluded from filing the form of bankruptcy that actually discharges debts (called Chapter 7) and instead be forced to use the form of bankruptcy that involves a repayment plan (called Chapter 13).

  Recognizing that folks living in higher cost-of-living areas tend to have higher incomes, the law allows for differences in income by making adjustments based upon your state of residence and family size. The expense side of the equation is considered as well, and allowances are determined by county and metropolitan area. I won't bore you with the details and required calculations here. Few potential filers are affected by this provision. For more information, click on the Means Testing Information section (`www.justice.gov/ust/means-testing`) on the U.S. Trustee's website (`www.justice.gov/ust`).
- **Increased requirements placed on filers and attorneys:** The means testing alone has created a good deal of additional work for bankruptcy filers, work generally done by attorneys. Filers, including lawyers, must also attest to the

accuracy of submitted information, which has attorneys doing more verification work. Thus, it's no surprise that when the new bankruptcy laws were passed, legal fees increased significantly — jumps of 30 to 40 percent were common.

» **New rules for people who recently moved:** Individual states have their own provisions for how much personal property and home equity you can keep. Prior to the passage of the current laws, in some cases, shortly before filing bankruptcy, people actually moved to a state that allowed them to keep more. Under the new law, you must live in the state for at least two years before filing bankruptcy in that state and using that state's personal property exemptions. To use a given state's *homestead exemption,* which dictates how much home equity you may protect, you must have lived in that state and owned a home for at least 40 months.

## Choosing between Chapter 7 and Chapter 13

You can file one of two forms of personal bankruptcy: Chapter 7 or Chapter 13. Here are the essentials regarding each type:

» **Chapter 7 bankruptcy allows you to discharge, or cancel, certain debts.** This form of bankruptcy makes the most sense when you have significant debts that you're legally allowed to cancel. (See "Understanding bankruptcy benefits" earlier in this chapter for details on which debts can be canceled, or discharged.)

» **Chapter 13 bankruptcy comes up with a repayment schedule that requires you to pay your debts over several years.** Chapter 13 stays on your credit record (just like Chapter 7), *but it doesn't eliminate debt,* so its value is limited — usually to dealing with debts like taxes that can't be discharged through bankruptcy. Chapter 13 can keep creditors at bay until you work out a repayment schedule in the courts.

## Seeking bankruptcy advice

TIP

If you want to find out more about the pros, cons, and details of filing for bankruptcy, pick up a copy of *The New Bankruptcy: Will It Work for You?* by attorney Cara O'Neill (Nolo Press). If you're comfortable with your decision to file and you think you can complete the paperwork, check out *How to File for Chapter 7 Bankruptcy*, by attorneys Albin Renauer and Cara O'Neill (Nolo Press), which comes with all the necessary filing forms.

# Stopping the Spending/Consumer Debt Cycle

Regardless of how you deal with paying off your debt, many folks are in real danger of falling back into old habits. Backsliding happens not only to people who file bankruptcy but also to those who use savings or home equity to eliminate their debt. This section speaks to that risk and tells you what to do about it.

## Resisting the credit temptation

Getting out of debt can be challenging, but I have confidence that you can do it with this book by your side. In addition to the ideas I discuss earlier in this chapter (such as eliminating all your credit cards and getting a debit card), the following list provides some additional tactics you can use to limit the influence credit cards hold over your life. (If you're concerned about the impact that any of these tactics may have on your credit rating, please see Chapter 6.)

TIP

- **Reduce your credit limit.** If you choose not to take my advice and get rid of all your credit cards or get a debit card, be sure to keep a lid on your credit card's *credit limit* (the maximum balance allowed on your card). You don't have to accept the increase just because your bank keeps raising your credit limit to reward you for being such a profitable customer. Call your credit card service's toll-free phone number and lower your credit limit to a level you're comfortable with.
- **Replace your credit card with a charge card.** A *charge card* (such as the American Express Card) requires you to pay your balance in full each billing period. You have no credit line or interest charges. Of course, spending more than you can afford to pay when the bill comes due is possible. But you'll be much less likely to overspend if you know you have to pay in full monthly.

- **Never buy anything on credit that depreciates in value.** Meals out, cars, clothing, and shoes all depreciate in value. Don't buy these things on credit. Borrow money only for sound investments — education that advances your career prospects, real estate, or your own business, for example.
- **Think in terms of total cost.** Everything sounds cheaper in terms of monthly payments — that's how salespeople entice you into buying things you can't afford. Take a calculator along, if necessary, to tally up the sticker price, interest charges, and upkeep. The total cost will scare you. *It should.*
- **Stop the junk mail avalanche.** Look at your daily mail — I bet half of it is solicitations and mail-order catalogs. You can save some trees and some time sorting junk mail by removing yourself from most mailing lists. To remove your name from mailing lists, contact the Direct Marketing Association (you can register through its website at `www.dmachoice.org/register.php`.) They now charge a $4 administrative fee for a ten-year registration period.

  To remove your name from the major credit reporting agency lists that are used by credit card solicitation companies, call 888-567-8688 or visit `www.optoutprescreen.com` online. Also, tell any credit card companies you keep cards with that you want your account marked to indicate that you don't want any of your personal information shared with telemarketing firms.
- **Limit what you can spend.** Go shopping with a small amount of cash and no plastic or checks. That way, you can spend only what little cash you have with you!

## Identifying and treating a compulsion

No matter how hard they try to break the habit, some people become addicted to spending and accumulating debt. It becomes a chronic problem that starts to interfere with other aspects of their lives and can lead to problems at work and with family and friends.

Debtors Anonymous (DA) is a nonprofit organization that provides support (primarily through group meetings) to people trying to break their debt accumulation and spending habits. DA is modeled after the 12-step Alcoholics Anonymous (AA) program.

Like AA, Debtors Anonymous works with people from all walks of life and socioeconomic backgrounds. You can find people who are financially on the edge, $100,000-plus income earners, and everybody in between at DA meetings. Even former millionaires join the program.

To find a Debtors Anonymous (DA) support group in your area, visit the DA website at www.debtorsanonymous.org or contact the DA's national headquarters by phone at 800-421-2383 or 781-453-2743.

IN THIS CHAPTER

» Choosing investment vehicles

» Determining your risk tolerance

» Diversifying your portfolio

# Chapter 5 Investment Strategies

Investing puts your money to work and is a cornerstone of financial literacy. Your investment choices should depend on where you're hoping to go, how fast you want to get there, and what risks you're willing to take. This chapter provides an overview of the basic investment vehicles you have to choose from. I also discuss risk tolerance and ways to diversify your investments.

## Understanding Investment Vehicles

The three best legal ways to build wealth are to invest in stocks (both domestic and international), real estate, and small business. That said, everyone should have some money in stable, safe investment vehicles, including money that you've earmarked for your near-term expenses, both expected and unexpected. Likewise, if you're saving money for a home purchase within the next few years, you certainly don't want to risk that money on the roller coaster of the stock market.

### Reducing risk with bonds

The investment option of bonds is appropriate for money you don't want to put at great risk. Bank accounts, discussed in Chapter 3, are also a safe place to save, but the returns tend to be lower.

When you invest in a bond, you effectively lend your money to an organization. When a bond is issued, it includes a specified maturity date at which time the principal will be repaid. Bonds are also issued at a particular interest rate, or what's known as a *coupon*. This rate is fixed on most bonds. So, for example, if you buy a five-year, 6-percent bond issued by Home Depot, you're lending your money to Home Depot for five years at an interest rate of 6 percent per year. (Bond interest is usually paid in two equal, semi-annual installments.)

The value of a bond generally moves opposite of the directional change in interest rates. For example, if you're holding a bond issued at 6 percent and rates on similar bonds increase to 8 percent, your 6-percent bond will decrease in value. (Why would anyone want to buy your bond at the price you paid if it yields just 6 percent and 8 percent can be obtained elsewhere?)

Some bonds are tied to variable interest rates. For example, you can buy bonds that are adjustable-rate mortgages, on which the interest rate can fluctuate. As an investor, you're actually lending your money to a mortgage borrower — indirectly, you're the banker making a loan to someone buying a home.

Bonds differ from one another in the following major ways:

- **The type of institution to which you're lending your money:** With municipal bonds, you lend your money to the state or local government or agency; with Treasuries, you lend your money to the federal government; with GNMAs (Ginnie Maes), you lend your money to a mortgage holder (and the federal government backs the bond); and with corporate bonds, you lend your money to a corporation.
- **The credit quality of the borrower to whom you lend your money:** Credit quality refers to the probability that the borrower will pay you the interest and return your principal as agreed.
- **The length of maturity of the bond:** Short-term bonds mature within a few years, intermediate bonds within 3 to 10 years, and long-term bonds within 10 to 30 years. Longer-term bonds generally pay higher yields but fluctuate more with changes in interest rates.

Some bonds are *callable,* which means that the bond's issuer can decide to pay you back earlier than the previously agreed-upon date. This event usually occurs when interest rates fall and the lender wants to issue new, lower-interest-rate bonds to replace the higher-rate, outstanding bonds. To compensate you for early repayment, the lender typically gives you a small premium over what the bond is currently valued at.

## Investing in stocks

*Stocks,* which represent shares of ownership in a company, are the most common ownership investment vehicle. When companies *go public,* they issue shares of stock that people like you and me can purchase on the major stock exchanges, such as the New York Stock Exchange and NASDAQ (National Association of Securities Dealers Automated Quotations).

As the economy grows and companies grow with it, earning greater profits, stock prices (and dividend payouts on those stocks) generally follow suit. Stock prices and dividends don't move in lockstep with earnings, but over the years, the relationship is pretty close. In fact, the *price-earnings ratio* — which measures the level of stock prices relative to (or divided by) company earnings — of U.S. stocks has averaged approximately 15 (although it has tended to be higher during periods of low inflation and interest rates). A price-earnings ratio of 15 simply means that stock prices per share, on average, are selling at about 15 times those companies' earnings per share.

Companies that issue stock (called *publicly held* companies) include automobile manufacturers, computer software producers, fast-food and other restaurant chains, hotels, publishers, supermarkets, technology companies, wineries, and everything in between! (You can also invest overseas — see the "Increasing opportunity with international stocks" section.) By contrast, some companies are *privately held,* which means that they've elected to have senior management and a small number of affluent investors own their stock. Privately held companies' stocks do not trade on a stock exchange, so folks like you and me can't buy stock in such firms.

REMEMBER

Investing in the stock market involves occasional setbacks and difficult moments (just like raising children or going mountain climbing), but the overall journey is almost certainly worth the effort. Over the past two centuries, the U.S. stock market has produced an annual average rate of return of about 9 percent. However, the market, as measured by the Dow Jones Industrial Average, fell more than 20 percent during 16 different periods in the 20th century. On average, these periods of decline lasted less than two years. So if you can withstand a temporary setback over a few years, the stock market is a proven place to invest for long-term growth.

You can invest in stocks by making your own selection of individual stocks or by letting mutual (or exchange-traded) funds do it for you.

## Choosing individual stocks

My experience is that plenty of people choose to invest in individual stocks because they think that they're smarter or luckier than the rest. I don't know you personally, but it's safe to say that in the long run, your investment choices are highly unlikely to outperform those of the best full-time investment professionals and index funds.

WARNING

Investing in individual stocks entails numerous drawbacks and pitfalls:

- **You need to spend a significant amount of time doing research.** When you're considering the purchase of an individual stock, you should understand a lot about the company in which you're thinking about investing. Relevant questions to ask about the company include the following:
  - What products or services does it sell?
  - What are its prospects for future growth and profitability?
  - How much debt does the company have?

  You need to do your homework not only before you make your initial investment but also on an ongoing basis for as long as you hold the investment. Research takes your valuable free time and sometimes costs money.
- **Your emotions will probably get in your way.** Analyzing financial statements, corporate strategy, and competitive position requires great intellect and insight. However, those skills aren't nearly enough. When your money is on the line, emotions often kick in and undermine your ability to make sound long-term decisions. Few people have the

psychological constitution to invest in individual stocks and handle and outfox the financial markets.

- **You're less likely to diversify.** Unless you have tens of thousands of dollars to invest in different stocks, you probably can't cost-effectively afford to research, develop, and monitor a diversified portfolio. By not diversifying, you unnecessarily add to your risk (see the section "Diversification: Not Just a Fancy Word for Variety" later in this chapter).
- **You'll face accounting and bookkeeping hassles.** When you invest in individual securities outside retirement accounts, every time you sell a specific security, you must report that transaction on your tax return. Even if you pay someone else to complete your tax return, you still have the hassle of keeping track of statements and receipts.

WARNING

Of course, you may find some people (with a vested interest) who try to convince you that picking your own stocks and managing your own portfolio of stocks is easy and more profitable than investing in, say, a mutual fund or an ETF. In my experience, such stock-picking cheerleaders are usually newsletter writers, book authors, or stockbrokers/investment advisors.

TIP

If you derive pleasure from picking and following your own stocks, or you want an independent opinion of some stocks you currently own, useful research reports are available from Value Line (call 800-825-8354 or visit `www.valueline.com`). I also recommend that you limit your individual stock holdings to no more than 20 percent of your overall investments.

## Increasing opportunity with international stocks

Not only can you invest in company stocks that trade on the U.S. stock exchanges, but you can also invest in stocks around the world. If you're in the United States, you may ask, "Why would you want to invest in international stocks?"

Here are two solid reasons:

- Many investing opportunities exist overseas. If you look at the total value of all stocks outstanding worldwide, the value of foreign stocks typically equals or exceeds the value of U.S. stocks.

- When you confine your investing to U.S. securities, you miss a world of opportunities, not only because of business growth available in other countries but also because you get the opportunity to diversify your portfolio even further.

International securities markets don't move in tandem with U.S. markets. During various U.S. stock market drops, some international stock markets drop less, whereas others may sometimes rise in value.

International investing managers generally look at opportunities in three major geographic regions:

- **Latin America:** Includes countries such as Argentina, Brazil, Chile, Columbia, Costa Rica, Mexico, Panama, and Peru.
- **Europe:** Includes countries such as Belgium, Denmark, France, Germany, Ireland, Italy, Netherlands, Norway, Spain, Sweden, Switzerland, and the United Kingdom.
- **Asia-Pacific:** Includes countries such as Australia, China, India, Japan, Hong Kong, India, New Zealand, Singapore, South Korea, Taiwan, Thailand, and Vietnam.

Companies in Canada are generally a small investment portion held by many international and global stock funds. Canadian holdings may be listed separately or as a part of North America holdings.

Another way in which foreign stocks are categorized is between developed markets and emerging markets.

- *Developed markets* are characterized by more mature, stable, and secure economies with relatively high standards of living. Examples include countries such as Australia, Canada, France, Germany, Japan, Switzerland, and the United Kingdom.
- *Emerging markets* tend to be more volatile and typically higher growth economies that are in their early economic stages. Examples include countries such as Brazil, China, Chile, India, Indonesia, Malaysia, Mexico, South Africa, and Thailand.

## Checking out mutual funds and exchange-traded funds

When you invest in a mutual fund or its close sibling — an exchange-traded fund (ETF) that trades on a stock exchange — an investment company pools your money with the money of many other individuals and invests it in stocks, bonds, and other securities. Think of it as a big investment club without the meetings! When you invest through a typical fund, several hundred million to billions of dollars are typically invested along with your money.

Mutual funds and exchange-traded funds (ETFs) rank right up there with microwave ovens, sticky notes, and cellphones as one of the best inventions. To understand their success is to grasp how and why these funds can work for you. Here are the benefits you receive when you invest in the best mutual funds and ETFs:

- **Professional management:** Mutual funds and ETFs are managed by a portfolio manager and research team whose full-time jobs are to screen the universe of investments for those that best meet the fund's stated objectives. These professionals call and visit companies, analyze companies' financial statements, and speak with companies' suppliers and customers. In short, the team does more research and analysis than you could ever hope to do in your free time.

  Fund managers are typically graduates of the top business and finance schools in the country, where they learn the principles of portfolio management and securities valuation and selection. The best fund managers typically have a decade or more of experience in analyzing and selecting investments, and many measure their experience in decades rather than years.
- **Low fees:** The most efficiently managed stock mutual funds and ETFs cost much less than 1 percent per year in fees (bond and money-market funds cost even less). And, when you buy a *no-load fund,* you avoid paying sales commissions (known as *loads*) on your transactions.
- **Diversification:** Fund investing enables you to achieve a level of diversification that's difficult to reach without tens of thousands of dollars and a lot of time to invest. Proper diversification allows a fund to receive the highest possible

return at the lowest possible risk given its objectives. To read more about diversification, see the section "Diversification: Not Just a Fancy Word for Variety" later in this chapter.

WARNING

If you go it alone, you should invest money in at least 15 to 20 different securities in different industries to ensure that your portfolio can withstand a downturn in one or more of the investments. The most unfortunate investors during major stock market downswings have been individuals who had all their money riding on only a few stocks that plunged in price by 90 percent or more.

- **Low cost of entry:** Most mutual funds have low minimum-investment requirements, especially for retirement account investors. (ETFs essentially have no minimum, although you don't want to do transactions involving small amounts if your brokerage firm charges a fee because that brokerage fee takes up a larger percentage of your investment amount.) Even if you have a lot of money to invest, consider funds for the low-cost, high-quality money-management services they provide.
- **Audited performance records and expenses:** In their prospectuses, all funds are required to disclose historical data on returns, operating expenses, and other fees. The U.S. Securities and Exchange Commission (SEC) and accounting firms check these disclosures for accuracy. Also, several firms (such as Morningstar and Value Line) report hundreds of fund statistics, allowing comparisons of performance, risk, and many other factors.
- **Flexibility in risk level:** Among the different funds, you can choose a level of risk that you're comfortable with and that meets your personal and financial goals. If you want your money to grow over a long period of time, you may want to select funds that invest more heavily in stocks. If you need current income and don't want investments that fluctuate in value as widely as stocks, you may choose more-conservative bond funds. If you want to be sure that your invested principal doesn't drop in value (perhaps because you may need your money in the short term), you can select a money-market fund.

The major types of funds are money-market, bond, and stock funds. When fund companies develop and market funds, the names they give their funds aren't always completely accurate or comprehensive. For example, a stock fund may not be *totally* invested in stocks. Twenty percent of it may be invested in bonds. Don't assume that a fund invests exclusively in U.S. companies, either — it may invest in international firms, as well.

REMEMBER

Efficiently managed mutual funds offer investors low-cost access to high-quality money managers. Mutual funds span the spectrum of risk and potential returns, from nonfluctuating money-market funds (which are similar to savings accounts) to bond funds (which generally pay higher yields than money-market funds but fluctuate with changes in interest rates) to stock funds (which offer the greatest potential for appreciation but also the greatest short-term volatility).

WARNING

Investing in individual securities should be done only by those who really enjoy doing it and are aware of and willing to accept the risks in doing so. Mutual funds and exchange-traded funds, if properly selected, are a low-cost, quality way to hire professional money managers. Over the long haul, you're highly unlikely to beat full-time professional managers who are investing in securities of the same type and at the same risk level.

The following sections cover the major fund types and a few others.

## Money-market funds

Money-market funds are generally considered the safest type of mutual funds (although not insured or guaranteed) for people concerned about losing their invested dollars. As with bank savings accounts, the value of your original investment does not fluctuate.

These funds are closely regulated by the SEC. Trillions of dollars of individuals' and institutions' money are invested in money-market funds. General-purpose money-market funds invest in safe, short-term bank certificates of deposit, U.S. Treasuries, and *corporate commercial paper* (short-term debt), which is issued by the largest and most creditworthy companies.

Money-market-fund investments can exist only in the most creditworthy securities and must have an average maturity of less than 120 days. In the unlikely event that an investment in a money-market-fund's portfolio goes sour, the mutual-fund company that stands behind the money-market fund will almost certainly cover the loss.

TIP

If the lack of insurance on money-market funds still spooks you, select a money-market fund that invests exclusively in U.S. government securities, which are virtually risk-free because they're backed by the full strength and credit of the federal government (as is the FDIC insurance system). These types of accounts typically pay slightly less interest, although the interest is free of state income tax.

## Bond funds

Bonds are IOUs. When you buy a newly issued bond, you typically lend your money to a corporation or government agency. A *bond fund* is nothing more than a large group of bonds.

Bond funds typically invest in bonds of similar *maturity* (the number of years that elapse before the borrower must pay back the money you lend). The names of most bond funds include a word or two that provides clues about the average length of maturity of their bonds. For example:

- A *short-term bond fund* typically concentrates its investments in bonds maturing in the next two to three years.
- An *intermediate-term fund* generally holds bonds that come due within three to ten years.
- The bonds in a *long-term fund* usually mature in more than ten years.

In contrast to an individual bond that you buy and hold until it matures, a bond fund is always replacing bonds in its portfolio to maintain its average maturity objective. Therefore, if you know that you absolutely, positively must have a certain principal amount back on a particular date, individual bonds may be more appropriate than a bond fund.

Like money-market funds, bond funds can invest in tax-free bonds, which are appropriate for investing money you hold outside retirement accounts if you're in a high tax bracket. (To find your tax bracket, see Chapter 9.)

TIP

Bond funds are useful when you want to live off interest income or you don't want to put all your money in riskier investments such as stocks and real estate (perhaps because you plan to use the money soon). Also, making small incremental investments in a bond fund is easier, as opposed to the cost of buying a single individual bond, which can be many thousands of dollars. Bonds (especially municipal bonds, which are bonds issued by local or state government) are among the most inefficient parts of the U.S. securities markets. Individual investors can't easily determine the bonds' true value and pay steep markups or markdowns, all of which a larger institutional trader (like a mutual fund) can more easily avoid.

## Stock funds

Stock funds, as their name implies, invest in stocks. These funds are often referred to as *equity funds*. *Equity* — not to be confused with equity in real estate — is another word for stocks. Stock funds are often categorized by the type of stocks they primarily invest in.

Stock types are first defined by size of company (small, medium, or large). The total market value *(capitalization)* of a company's outstanding stock determines its size. Small-company stocks, for example, are usually defined as companies with total market capitalization of less than $2 billion. Mid-cap stocks are defined as having a market capitalization of between $2 and $10 billion, and large cap stocks are those with market caps over $10 billion. Stocks are further categorized as growth or value stocks:

- **Growth stocks** represent companies that are experiencing rapidly expanding revenues and profits and typically have high stock prices relative to their current earnings or asset (book) values. These companies tend to reinvest most of their earnings in their infrastructure to fuel future expansion. Thus, growth stocks typically pay low dividends.
- **Value stocks** are at the other end of the spectrum. Value stock investors look for good buys. They want to invest in stocks that are cheaply priced in relation to the profits per share and book value (assets less liabilities) of the company. Value stocks are usually less volatile than growth stocks.

These categories are combined in various ways to describe how a mutual fund invests its money. One fund may focus on large-company growth stocks, while another fund may limit itself to small-company value stocks. Funds are further classified by the geographical focus of their investments: U.S., international, worldwide, and so on (see the later section "U.S., international, and global funds").

## Balanced funds: Mixing bonds and stocks

*Balanced funds* invest in a mixture of different types of securities. Most commonly, they invest in bonds and stocks. These funds are usually less risky and volatile than funds that invest exclusively in stocks. In an economic downturn, bonds usually hold up in value better than stocks do. However, during good economic times when the stock market is booming, the bond portions of these funds tend to drag down their performance a bit.

Balanced mutual funds generally try to maintain a fairly constant percentage of investments in stocks and bonds. A similar class of funds, known as *asset allocation funds,* tends to adjust the mix of different investments according to the portfolio manager's expectations of the market. Of course, exceptions do exist — some balanced funds adjust their allocations, whereas some asset allocation funds maintain a relatively fixed mix.

REMEMBER

Most funds that shift money around instead of staying put in good investments rarely beat the market averages over a number of years.

There are now also increasing numbers of target-date or retirement-date funds, which tend to decrease their risk (and stock allocation) over time. Such funds appeal to investors who are approaching a particular future goal, such as retirement or a child's college education, and want their fund to automatically adjust as that date approaches.

TIP

Balanced funds are a way to make fund investing simple. They give you extensive diversification across a variety of investing options. They also make it easier for stock-skittish investors to invest in stocks while avoiding the high volatility of pure stock funds.

## U.S., international, and global funds

Unless they have words like *international, global, worldwide,* or *world* in their names, most American-issued funds focus their investments in the United States. But even funds without one of these terms attached may invest some of their money internationally.

TIP

The only way to know for sure where a fund is currently invested (or where the fund may invest in the future) is to investigate. A fund's annual report (which can be found on the fund company's website) details where the fund is investing (the prospectus also details where the fund can be invested). You can also call the toll-free number of the fund company you're interested in and ask.

When a fund has the term *international* or *foreign* in its name, it typically means that the fund invests anywhere in the world *except* the United States. The term *worldwide* or *global* generally implies that a fund invests everywhere in the world, *including* the United States.

### Index funds

*Index funds* are funds that can be (and are, for the most part) managed by a formulaic approach. An index fund's assets are invested to replicate an existing market index such as Standard & Poor's 500, an index of 500 large U.S. company stocks. (Some exchange-traded funds are index funds with the added twist that they trade on a major stock exchange.)

Over long periods (ten years or more), index funds outperform about three-quarters of their peers! How is that possible? How can mindlessly mimicking the holdings of a given index beat an intelligent, creative, MBA-endowed portfolio manager with a crack team of research analysts scouring the market for the best securities? The answer is largely cost. You can run an index fund with a much smaller management team and without spending gobs of money on research. An index fund doesn't need a team of research analysts.

In contrast to passively managed index funds, most active fund managers can't overcome the handicap of high operating expenses that pull down their funds' rates of return. Operating expenses include all the fees and profit that a mutual fund extracts from a fund's returns before the returns are paid to you. For example, the average U.S. stock fund has an operating expense ratio of 1.1 percent per year. So a U.S. stock index fund (or its peer exchange-traded fund, which is an index fund that trades on a stock exchange) with an expense ratio of just 0.1 percent per year has an advantage of 1.0 percent per year.

Another not-so-inconsequential advantage of index funds is that they can't underperform the market. Many actively managed funds do just that because of the burden of high fees and/or poor management. For money invested outside retirement accounts, index funds have an added advantage: Lower taxable capital gains distributions are made to shareholders because less trading of securities is conducted and a more stable portfolio is maintained.

Yes, index funds may seem downright boring. When you invest in them, you give up the opportunity to brag to others about your shrewd investments that beat the market averages. On the other hand, with a low-cost index fund, you have no chance of doing worse than the market (which plenty of active investment managers do).

TIP

Index funds and exchange-traded funds make sense for a portion of your investments, because beating the market is difficult for portfolio managers. The Vanguard Group (phone 800-662-7447; website www.vanguard.com), headquartered in Valley Forge, Pennsylvania, is the largest and lowest-cost provider of such funds.

### Exchange-traded funds (ETFs)

These funds are much like mutual funds except that they trade on a major stock exchange and thus can be bought and sold during the trading day. The best ETFs have low fees and, like an index fund, invest to track the performance of a particular stock market index.

### Hedge funds

These privately managed funds are for wealthier investors and are generally riskier (some even go bankrupt) than a typical mutual fund. The fees can be steep — typically 15 to 20 percent of the hedge fund's annual returns as well as an annual management fee of 1 percent or so. They're also generally illiquid — there are usually lock-up periods, and it can still be difficult to get your money back out later when needed. I generally don't recommend them.

### Managed accounts

The major brokerage firms, which employ brokers on commission, offer access to private money managers. In reality, this option isn't really different from getting access to fund managers via mutual funds, but you'll generally pay a much higher fee, which reduces this option's attractiveness.

## Specialty (sector) funds

Specialty funds don't fit neatly into the previous categories. These funds are often known as *sector funds*, because they generally invest in securities in specific industries.

WARNING

In most cases, you should avoid investing in specialty funds. Investing in stocks of a single industry defeats one of the major purposes of investing in funds — diversification. Another good reason to avoid specialty funds is that they tend to carry higher expenses than other funds.

TIP

Specialty funds that invest in real estate or precious metals may make sense for a small portion (10 percent or less) of your investment portfolio. These types of funds can help diversify your portfolio, because they can do better during times of higher inflation.

# Deciding whether real-estate investing is for you

Although real estate is unique in some ways, it's also like other types of investments in that prices are driven by supply and demand. You can invest in homes or small apartment buildings and then rent them out. In the long run, investment-property buyers hope that their rental income and the value of their properties will increase faster than their expenses.

When selecting real estate for investment purposes, remember that local economic growth is the fuel for housing demand. In addition to a vibrant and diverse job base, you want to look for limited supplies of both existing housing and land on which to build. When you identify potential properties in which you may want to invest, run the numbers to understand the cash demands of owning the property and the likely profitability.

Real estate differs from most other investments in several respects. Here's what makes real estate unique as an investment:

- **You can live in it.** Real estate is the only investment you can use (by living in it or renting it out) to produce income.
- **Land is in limited supply.** The demand for land and housing continues to grow. Consider the areas that have the most expensive real-estate prices in the world — Hong Kong,

Tokyo, Hawaii, San Francisco, and Manhattan. In these densely populated areas, little if any new land is available for building new housing.

- **Zoning shapes potential value.** Local government regulates the zoning of property, and zoning determines what a property can be used for. In most communities these days, local zoning boards are against big growth. This position bodes well for future real-estate values. Also know that in some cases, a particular property may not have been developed to its full potential. If you can figure out how to better develop the property, you can reap greater profits.
- **You don't need a lot of cash up front.** Real estate is also different from other investments because you can borrow a lot of money to buy it — up to 80 to 90 percent or more of the value of the property. This borrowing is known as exercising *leverage:* With only a small investment of 10 to 20 percent down, you're able to purchase and own a much larger investment. When the value of your real estate goes up, you make money on your investment and on all the money you borrowed.
- **You can discover hidden value.** In an *efficient market,* the price of an investment accurately reflects its true worth. Some investment markets are more efficient than others because of the large number of transactions and easily accessible information. Real-estate markets can be inefficient at times. Information is not always easy to come by, and you may find an ultra-motivated or uninformed seller. If you're willing to do some homework, you may be able to purchase a property below its fair market value (perhaps by as much as 10 to 20 percent).

TIP

Buying your own home is the best place to start investing in real estate. The *equity* (the difference between the market value of the home and the loan owed on it) in your home that builds over the years can become a significant part of your net worth. Among other things, you can tap this equity to help finance other important personal goals, such as retirement, higher-education costs, and starting or buying a business. Moreover, throughout your adult life, owning a home should be less expensive than renting a comparable home.

## Drawbacks of real-estate investing

Just as with any other investment, real estate has its drawbacks. For starters, buying or selling a property generally takes time and incurs significant cost. When you're renting property, you discover firsthand the occasional headaches of being a landlord. And especially in the early years of rental property ownership, the property's expenses may exceed the rental income, producing a net cash drain.

If you don't want to be a landlord — one of the biggest drawbacks of investment real estate — consider investing in real estate through real-estate investment trusts (REITs). *REITs* are diversified real-estate investment companies that purchase and manage rental real estate for investors. A typical REIT invests in one or two types of property, such as shopping centers, apartments, and other rental buildings. You can invest in REITs either by purchasing them directly on the major stock exchanges or by investing in a real-estate mutual fund that invests in numerous REITs.

REMEMBER

When investing in real estate, you earn no tax benefits while you're accumulating your down payment. Retirement accounts such as 401(k)s, SEP-IRAs, 403(b)s, and so on give you an immediate tax deduction as you contribute money to them. If you haven't exhausted your tax-deductible contributions to these accounts, consider doing so before chasing after investment real estate.

## Bad real-estate investments

WARNING

Not all real-estate investments are good; some aren't even real investments. The bad ones are characterized by burdensome costs and problematic economic fundamentals:

- **Limited partnerships:** Avoid limited partnerships (LPs) sold through brokers and financial consultants. LPs are inferior investment vehicles. They're overly burdened with high sales commissions and ongoing management fees that deplete your investment; you can do better elsewhere. The investment salesperson who sells you such an investment stands to earn a commission of up to 10 percent or more — so only 90 cents of each dollar gets invested. Each year, LPs typically siphon off another several percent for management and other expenses. Most partnerships have little or no incentive to control costs. In fact, they have a conflict of interest that forces them to charge more to enrich the managing partners.

Unlike a mutual fund, you can't vote with your dollars. If the partnership is poorly run and expensive, you're stuck. LPs are *illiquid* (not readily convertible into cash without a substantial loss). You can't access your money until the partnership is liquidated, typically seven to ten years after you buy in.

Many of the yields on LPs have turned out to be bogus. In some cases, partnerships prop up their yields by paying back investors' principals (without telling them, of course). As for returns — well — historically, too many LPs have been turkeys. The only thing limited about a limited partnership is its ability to make you money.

- **Time-shares:** Time-shares are another nearly certain money loser. With a time-share, you buy a week or two of ownership, or usage, of a particular unit (usually a condominium in a resort location) per year. If, for example, you pay $12,000 for a week (in addition to ongoing maintenance fees), you're paying the equivalent of more than $600,000 for the whole unit, when a comparable unit nearby may sell for only $225,000. The extra markup pays the salespeople's commissions, administrative expenses, and profits for the time-share development company.

  If you can't live without a time-share, consider buying a used one. Many previous buyers, who more than likely have lost a good chunk of money, are trying to dump their shares (which should tell you something).

- **Second homes:** The weekend getaway is a sometimes romantic notion and an extended part of the so-called American dream. When your vacation home is not in use, you may be able to rent it out and earn some income to help defray the expense of keeping it up. However, most second-home owners seldom rent out their property — they typically do so 10 percent or less of the time. As a result, second homes are usually money drains, not investments.

  The supposed tax benefits are part of the attraction of a second home. Even when you qualify for some or all of them, tax benefits only partially reduce the cost of owning a property. In some cases, the second home is such a cash drain that it prevents its owners from contributing to and taking advantage of tax-deductible retirement savings plans.

If you aren't going to rent out a second home most of the time, ask yourself whether you can afford such a luxury. Can you accomplish your other financial goals — saving for retirement, paying for the home in which you live, and so on — with this added expense? Keeping a second home is more of a consumption than an investment decision. Few people can afford more than one home.

## Building wealth through small business investing

**Small business is the leading investment through which folks have built the greatest wealth. Here are some options to consider:**

- **Launching your own enterprise.** Of all the small-business investment options, starting your own business involves the most work. Although you can do this work on a part-time basis in the beginning, most people end up running their business full-time — it's your new job, career, or whatever you want to call it. When you have self-discipline and a product or service you can sell, starting your own business can be both profitable and fulfilling.

  **Buying an existing business.** Finding and buying a good small business takes much time and patience, so be willing to devote at least several months to the search. You may also need to enlist financial and legal advisors to help inspect the company, look over its financial statements, and hammer out a contract. Although you don't have to go through the riskier start-up period if you buy a small business, you'll likely need more capital to buy an established enterprise.

  TIP

  Purchasing a good franchise can be another way to "buy an existing business." When you purchase a franchise, you buy the local rights to a specified geographic territory to sell a company's products or services under the company's name and to use the company's system of operation. In addition to an up-front franchisee fee, franchisers also typically charge an ongoing royalty.

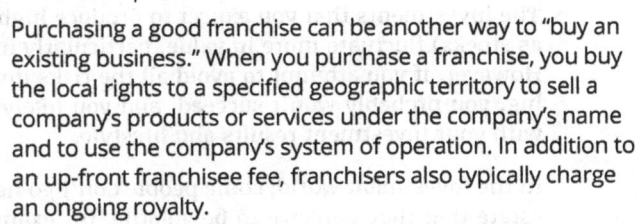

- **Investing in someone else's small business.** The best private companies who are seeking investors generally don't advertise. Instead, they find prospective investors through networking with people such as business advisors. Also, private firms aren't required to produce comprehensive, audited financial statements that adhere to certain accounting principles. Thus, you have a greater risk of not having sufficient or accurate information when evaluating a small, private firm.

You can increase your chances of finding private companies to invest in by speaking with tax, legal, and financial advisors who work with small businesses. You can also find interesting opportunities through your own contacts or experience within a given industry.

WARNING

Don't consider investing in someone else's business unless you can afford to lose all of what you're investing. Also, you should have sufficient assets so that what you're investing in small, privately held companies represents only a small portion (20 percent or less) of your total financial assets.

## Are You a Daredevil or a Safety Net Enthusiast?

Who among us wants to lose money? Of course you don't! You put your money into an investment in the hope and expectation that you will get back more in total than you put in. And you'd rather your chosen investments not fluctuate too widely in value. When it comes to financial literacy regarding investing, no concepts are more important to grasp than *risk* and *return*, which I explain in this section.

### Realizing risks

The investments that you expect to produce higher returns (such as stocks) fluctuate more in value, particularly in the short term. However, if you attempt to avoid all the risks involved in investing, you probably won't succeed, and you likely won't be happy with your investment results and lifestyle.

In the investment world, some people don't go near stocks or real estate that they perceive to be volatile, for example. As a result, such investors often end up with lousy long-term returns and expose themselves to some high risks that they overlooked, such as the risk of inflation and taxes eroding the purchasing power of their money.

You can't live without taking risks. Risk-free activities or ways of living don't exist. You can sensibly minimize risks, but you can never eliminate them. Some methods of risk reduction aren't palatable because they reduce your quality of life.

Risks are also composed of several factors. Following are the major types of investment risks and a few of the methods you can use to reduce these risks while not missing out on the upside that investments offer:

- **Market-value risk:** Although stocks can help you build wealth, they can also drop 20 percent or more in a relatively short period of time. Entering 2020, who was thinking about how a pandemic and the government's response may impact stock prices? Then, in a few weeks, stocks slid more than 30 percent due to government-mandated economic shutdowns. Although real estate, like stocks, has been a rewarding long-term investment, various real-estate markets get clobbered from time to time.
- **Individual-investment risk:** A down market can put an entire investment market on a roller-coaster ride, but healthy markets also have their share of individual losers. Just as individual stock prices can plummet, so can individual real-estate property prices.

  WARNING

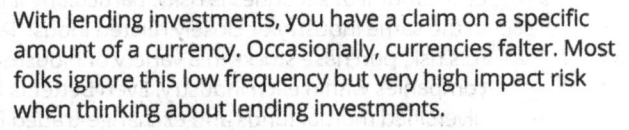

  With lending investments, you have a claim on a specific amount of a currency. Occasionally, currencies falter. Most folks ignore this low frequency but very high impact risk when thinking about lending investments.
- **Purchasing-power risk:** *Inflation* — which is an increase in the cost of living — can erode the value of your money and its *purchasing power* (what you can buy with that money). Skittish investors often keep their money in bonds and money-market accounts, thinking that they're playing it safe. The risk in this strategy is that your money won't grow enough over the years for you to accomplish your financial goals. In other words, the lower the return you earn, the more you need to save to reach a financial goal.
- **Liquidity risk:** Some investments are more *liquid* (how quickly an investment can be converted to cash) than others and more readily sold at fair market value on short notice. Bank savings accounts have no real liquidity risk. A real-estate investment, by contrast, takes time and money to sell,

and if you must sell most real estate quickly, you'll likely get a fair amount less than its current full market value.

- **Career risk:** In your 20s and 30s, your ability to earn money is probably your biggest asset. Education is a lifelong process. If you don't periodically invest in your education, you risk losing your competitive edge. Your skills and perspectives can become dated and obsolete. Although that doesn't mean you should work 80 hours a week and never do anything fun, it does mean that part of your "work" time should involve upgrading your skills.

## Managing risks

Here are some simple steps you can take to lower the risk of investments that can upset the achievement of your goals:

- **Do your homework.** When you purchase real estate, various inspections, for example, can save you from buying a money pit. With stocks, you can examine some measures of value and the company's financial condition and business strategy to reduce your chances of buying into an overpriced company or one on the verge of major problems.
- **Diversify.** Placing significant amounts of your capital in one or a handful of securities is risky, particularly if the stocks are in the same industry or closely related industries. To reduce this risk, purchase stocks in a variety of industries and companies within each industry. Even better is buying diversified mutual funds and exchange-traded funds.

  Diversifying your investments can involve more than just your stock portfolio. You can also hold some real-estate investments to diversify your investment portfolio. See the section "Diversification: Not Just a Fancy Word for Variety" later in this chapter.

TIP

If you worry about the health of the U.S. economy, the government, and the dollar, you can reduce your overall investment risk by also investing overseas so that you have a globally diversified portfolio of stocks. Most large U.S. companies do business overseas, so when you invest in larger U.S. company stocks, you get some international investment exposure. You can also invest in international company stocks, ideally through funds.

- **Minimize holdings in costly markets.** Although I don't believe that most investors can time the markets — buy low, sell high — spotting a greatly overpriced market isn't too difficult. You should avoid overpriced investments because when they fall, they usually fall farther and faster than more fairly priced investments. Also, you should be able to find other investments that offer higher potential returns.
- **View market declines in a different light.** Instead of seeing declines and market corrections as horrible things, view them as potential opportunities or "sales." If you pass up the stock and real-estate markets simply because of the potential market-value risk, you miss out on a historic, time-tested method of building substantial wealth. Try not to give in to the human emotions that often scare people away from buying something that others seem to be shunning.

## Making sense of returns

Each investment has its own mix of associated risks that you take when you part with your investment dollar and, likewise, offers a different potential rate of return. When you make investments, you have the potential to make money in a variety of ways.

To determine how much money you've made or lost on your investment, you calculate the total return. To come up with this figure, you determine how much money you originally invested and then factor in the other components, such as interest, dividends, and appreciation or depreciation.

If you've ever had money in a bank account that pays interest, you know that the bank pays you a small amount of interest in exchange for your allowing the bank to keep your money. The bank then turns around and lends your money to some other person or organization at a much higher rate of interest. The rate of interest is also known as the *yield.* So if a bank tells you that its savings account pays 1.5 percent interest, the bank may also say that the account yields 1.5 percent. Banks usually quote interest rates or yields on an annual basis. Interest that you receive is one component of the return you receive on your investment.

If a bank pays monthly interest, the bank also likely quotes a compounded effective annual yield. After the first month's interest is credited to your account, that interest starts earning interest as well. So the bank may say that the account pays 1.5 percent, which compounds to an effective annual yield of 1.53 percent.

When you lend your money directly to a company — which is what you do when you invest in a bond that a corporation issues — you also receive interest. Bonds, as well as stocks (which are shares of ownership in a company), fluctuate in market value after they're issued.

When you invest in a company's stock, you hope that the stock increases (appreciates) in value. Of course, a stock can also decline, or depreciate, in value. This change in market value is part of your return from a stock or bond investment.

Stocks can also pay dividends, which are the company's way of sharing some of its profits with you as a stockholder and thus are part of your return. Some companies, particularly those that are small or growing rapidly, choose to reinvest all their profits back into the company.

REMEMBER

Unless you held your investments in a tax-sheltered retirement account, you owe taxes on your return. Specifically, the dividends and investment appreciation that you realize upon selling are taxed, although often at relatively low rates. The tax rates on so-called long-term capital gains and stock dividends are currently and historically lower than the tax rates on other income.

## Matching risk-taking to your investment goals

With money that you're investing for shorter-term goals, you have a more limited menu of investments to choose from. For your emergency/rainy-day fund, for example, you should consider only a money-market fund or bank/credit union savings account. Down-payment money for a home purchase that you expect to make in a few years should be kept in short-term bonds.

When you're younger and have more years until you plan to use your money, you should keep larger amounts of your long-term investment money in growth (ownership) investments, such as stocks, real estate, and small business. The attraction of these types of investments is their potential to really grow your money, but the risk is that the value of such investments can fall significantly.

The younger you are, the more time your investments have to recover from a bad fall. A long-held guiding principle says to subtract your age from 110 and invest the resulting number as a percentage of money to place in growth (ownership) investments. So if you're 30 years old, 110 – 30 = 80 percent in growth investments.

Should you want to be more conservative, subtract your age from 100: 100 – 30 = 70 percent in growth investments.

Want to be even more aggressive? Subtract your age from 120: 120 – 30 = 90 percent in growth investments.

REMEMBER

These guidelines are general ones that apply to money that you invest for the long term (ideally, for ten years or more). In your younger adult years, you can consider investing all of your money in retirement accounts in stocks and stock funds given the long time frame you have with such accounts.

## Diversification: Not Just a Fancy Word for Variety

*Diversification* is one of the most powerful investment concepts. It refers to saving your eggs (or investments) in different baskets. Diversification requires you to place your money in different investments with returns that are not completely correlated, which is a fancy way of saying that when some of your investments are down in value, odds are that others are up in value.

TIP

To decrease the chances of all your investments getting clobbered at the same time, you must put your money in different types of investments, such as bonds, stocks, real estate, and small business. You can further diversify your investments by investing in domestic as well as international markets.

Within a given class of investments, such as stocks, investing in different types of that class (such as different types of stocks) that perform well under various economic conditions is important. For this reason, *mutual funds,* which are diversified portfolios of securities such as stocks or bonds, are a highly useful investment vehicle, as are exchange-traded funds (ETFs), which are like mutual funds but trade on a stock exchange. When you buy into a mutual fund, your money is pooled with the money of many others and invested in a vast array of stocks or bonds.

You can look at the benefits of diversification in two ways:

- » Diversification reduces the volatility in the value of your whole portfolio. In other words, your portfolio can achieve the same rate of return that a single investment can provide with less fluctuation in value.
- » Diversification allows you to obtain a higher rate of return for a given level of risk.

REMEMBER

Keep in mind that no one, no matter whom they work for or what credentials they have, can guarantee returns on an investment. You can do good research and get lucky, but no one is free from the risk of losing money. Diversification allows you to hedge the risk of your investments.

## Allocating your assets

*Asset allocation* refers to how you spread your investing dollars among different investment choices (stocks, bonds, money-market accounts, and so on). Before you can intelligently decide how to allocate your assets, you need to ponder a number of issues, including your present financial situation, your goals and priorities, and the pros and cons of various investment alternatives.

Although stocks and real estate offer attractive long-term returns, they can sometimes suffer significant declines. Thus, these investments are not suitable for money that you think you may want or need to use within, say, the next five years.

TIP

Money-market and shorter-term bond investments are good places to keep money that you expect to use soon. Everyone should have a reserve of money — about three to six months' worth of living expenses in a money-market fund — that's accessible in an emergency. Shorter-term bonds or bond mutual funds can serve as a higher-yielding, secondary emergency cushion. (See Chapter 2 for more on emergency reserves.)

TIP

Bonds can also be useful for some longer-term investing for diversification purposes. For example, when investing for retirement, placing a portion of your money in bonds helps buffer stock market declines.

## Allocating money for the long term

Investing money for retirement is a classic long-term goal for most people. Your current age and the number of years until you expect to need the money and retire are the biggest factors to consider when allocating money for long-term purposes. The younger you are and the more years you have before retirement, the more comfortable you can afford to be with growth-oriented (and more volatile) investments, such as stocks and investment real estate.

TIP

One useful guideline for dividing or allocating your money between longer-term-oriented growth investments, such as stocks, and more-conservative lending investments, such as bonds, is to subtract your age from 110 (or 120 if you want to be aggressive; 100 to be more conservative) and invest the resulting percentage in stocks. You then invest the remaining amount in bonds. For example, if you're 30 years old, you invest from 70 (100 – 30) to 90 (120 – 30) percent in stocks. You invest the remaining 10 to 30 percent in bonds.

Table 5-1 lists some guidelines for allocating long-term money based on your age and the level of risk you desire.

**TABLE 5-1 Allocating Long-Term Money**

| Your Investment Attitude | Bond Allocation (%) | Stock Allocation (%) |
|---|---|---|
| Play it safer | = Age | = 100 – age |
| Middle-of-the-road | = Age – 10 | = 110 – age |
| Aggressive | = Age – 20 | = 120 – age |

For example, if you're the conservative sort who doesn't like a lot of risk but recognizes the value of striving for some growth and making your money work harder, you're a *middle-of-the-road* type. Using Table 5-1, if you're 40 years old, you may consider putting 30 percent (40 – 10) in bonds and 70 percent (110 – 40) in stocks.

TIP

In most employer retirement plans, mutual funds are the typical investment vehicle. If all your retirement plan's stock fund options are good, you can simply divide your stock allocation among the choices. When one or more of the choices is an international stock fund, consider allocating a percentage of your stock fund money to overseas investments: at least 20 percent for play-it-safe investors, 25 to 35 percent for middle-of-the-road investors, and as much as 35 to 50 percent for aggressive investors.

If the 40-year-old middle-of-the-roader from the previous example is investing 70 percent in stocks, about 25 to 35 percent of the stock fund investments (which works out to be about 18 to 24 percent of the total) can be invested in international stock funds.

## Resisting the urge to trade

Your goals and desire to take risk should drive the allocation of your investment dollars. As you get older, gradually scaling back on the riskiness (and therefore growth potential and volatility) of your portfolio generally makes sense.

Don't tinker with your portfolio daily, weekly, monthly, or even annually. (Every two to three years or so, you may want to rebalance your holdings to get your mix to a desired asset allocation, as I discuss in the preceding section.) Don't engage in trading with the hopes of buying into a hot investment and selling your losers. Jumping onto a "winner" and dumping a "loser" may provide some short-term psychological comfort, but in the long term, such an investment strategy often produces below-average returns.

WARNING

When an investment gets front-page coverage and everyone is talking about its stunning rise, it's definitely time to take a reality check. The higher an investment's price rises, the greater the danger that it's overpriced. Its next move may be downward. Don't follow the herd.

During the late 1990s, many technology (especially internet) stocks had spectacular rises, thus attracting a lot of attention. However, the fact that the U.S. economy is increasingly becoming technology-based doesn't mean that any price you pay for a technology stock is fine. Some investors who neglected to do basic research and bought into the attention-grabbing, high-flying technology stocks lost 80 percent or more of their investments in the early 2000s — ouch! The same pattern repeated itself in 2022 in the aftermath of the pandemic and the rapid price rise of numerous technology stocks that then got clobbered.

Conversely, when things look bleak (as when stocks in general suffered significant losses in the early 2000s and then again in the late 2000s and early 2020), giving up hope is easy — who wants to be associated with a loser? However, investors who forget about their overall asset allocation plan, panic, and sell *after* a major decline miss out on a tremendous buying opportunity.

Many people like buying everything from clothing to cars to chicken on sale — yet whenever the stock market has a clearance sale, most investors stampede for the exits instead of snatching up great buys. Demonstrate your courage; again, don't follow the herd.

## Investing lump sums via dollar-cost averaging

When you have what is to you a large chunk of cash to invest — whether you received it from an accumulation of funds over the years, an inheritance, or a recent windfall from work you've done — you may have a problem deciding what to do with it. Many people, of course, would like to have your problem. (You're not complaining, right?) You want to invest your money, but you're a bit skittish — if not outright terrified — at the prospect of investing the lump of money all at once.

REMEMBER

If the money is residing in a savings or money-market account, you may feel like it's wasting away. You want to put it to work! My first words of advice are "Don't rush." Nothing is wrong with earning a small return in a money-market account. Remember that a money-market fund beats the heck out of rushing into an investment in which you may lose 20 percent or more.

TIP

Take a deep breath. You have absolutely no reason to rush into an important decision. Tell your friendly banker that when the CD matures, you want to put the proceeds into the bank's highest-yielding savings or money-market account. That way, your money continues to earn interest while you buy yourself some breathing room.

One approach to investing is called *dollar-cost averaging* (DCA). With DCA, you invest your money in equal chunks on a regular basis — such as once a month — into a diversified group of investments. For example, if you have $60,000 to invest, you can invest $2,500 per month until it's all invested, which takes a couple of years. The money awaiting future investment isn't lying fallow; you keep it in a money-market account so it can earn a bit of interest while waiting its turn.

The attraction of DCA is that it allows you to ease into riskier investments instead of jumping in all at once. If the price of the investment drops after some of your initial purchases, you can buy some later at a lower price. If you dump your entire chunk of money into an investment all at once and then it drops like a stone, you'll be kicking yourself for not waiting.

The flip side of DCA is that when your investment of choice appreciates in value, you may wish that you had invested your money faster. Another drawback of DCA is that you may get cold feet as you continue to pour money into an investment that's dropping in value.

DCA can also cause headaches with your taxes when the time comes to sell investments held outside retirement accounts. When you buy an investment at many different times and prices, the accounting becomes muddied as you sell blocks of the investment.

TIP

DCA is most valuable when the money you want to invest represents a large portion of your total assets and you can stick to a schedule. Make DCA automatic so you're less likely to abandon plans if the investment falls after your initial purchases. Look for investment firms that provide automatic exchange services (investing a set amount at regular intervals, such as monthly, drafting the money from a bank account or money fund).

IN THIS CHAPTER

» Seeing how lenders use credit reporting and credit scores

» Reviewing your credit reports and correcting errors

» Obtaining and interpreting your credit score

» Improving your credit rating

# Chapter 6 Credit Scores and Reports: The Magic Numbers

Most people borrow money at various times in their life, whether it's to buy a home (or other real estate), to finance a small business, to pay for educational expenses, or for other purposes. If you expect to apply for a loan of any type and get a competitively low interest rate, you should understand your credit report and credit score and how to improve each.

## Why Your Credit Report and Credit Score Matter

A *credit report* is basically your credit history, while a *credit score* is a three-digit score based on the information in your personal credit report. When you want to borrow money, lenders examine your credit report and your credit score(s) to determine how responsible you've been in the past with credit and to help them decide whether they should lend you money (and if so, how much to charge you based on your past behavior with credit).

Specifically, lenders examine your history of credit usage in your credit report. This information tells the lender when each of your accounts was opened, what the recent balance is, your track record of making payments on time, and whether you've defaulted on any loans. A credit report also tells a prospective lender where else you've been applying for credit most recently.

Lenders use your credit score to help them predict the likelihood that you'll default on repaying a loan. The higher your credit score the better, because a high credit score means that you have a lower likelihood of defaulting on a loan. Thus, more lenders will be willing to extend you credit and charge you lower rates for that credit.

TIP

A high credit score puts you in a negotiating position to ask for better rates. Lenders are in the moneymaking business, and many don't automatically give you the best rate for which you qualify.

## Making Sense of Credit Reports

An important part of financial literacy involves staying on top of your credit reports. This section shows how to obtain and review your credit reports, and address any errors you uncover.

A *credit report* contains information such as

- **Personal identifying information:** Includes your name, address, Social Security number, and so on
- **Record of credit accounts:** Details when each account was opened, the latest balance, your payment history, and so on
- **Bankruptcy filings:** Indicates whether you've filed bankruptcy in recent years. Chapter 7 can stay on your credit report for ten years, and Chapter 13 for seven years.
- **Inquiries:** Lists who has accessed your credit report because you applied for credit

REMEMBER

Your credit reports do *not* include your credit score. Thus, if you want to obtain your credit score, it's going to cost you. See the section "Getting Your Credit Score" later in this chapter.

## Obtaining your credit reports

You're entitled to receive a free copy of your credit report (which does *not* contain your credit score) every 12 months from each of the three credit bureaus — Equifax, Experian, and TransUnion.

If you visit www.annualcreditreport.com, you can view and print copies of your credit report from each of the three credit agencies. (Alternatively, you can call 877-322-8228 and request that your reports be mailed to you.) You may want to order your credit report from a different bureau every four months rather than getting all three at once.

## Reviewing your credit reports

When you obtain your reports, inspect them for possible mistakes. You want to correct any mistakes because they can adversely affect your credit score. Credit-reporting bureaus and the creditors who report credit information to these bureaus make some errors.

If your problems are fixable, there's no need to hire someone to take care of it for you — you can fix them yourself, but you will likely have to make some phone calls or submit a dispute online or by writing a letter or two. (See the next section, "Fixing credit-report errors," for more details on fixing errors.)

Some credit-report errors arise from other people's negative information getting on your credit report. This can happen if you have a common name, have moved a lot, or for other reasons. If the problematic information on your report appears not to be yours, tell that particular credit bureau and explain that you need more information because you don't recognize the creditor.

## Fixing credit-report errors

If you obtain your credit report and find a blemish on it that you don't recognize as being your mistake or fault, do *not* assume that the information is correct.

You're going to have to fill out a form on a website, make some phone calls, or write a letter or two to fix the problems on your credit report. Here's how to correct most errors that aren't your fault:

- **If the credit problem is someone else's:** A surprising number of personal credit-report glitches are the result of someone else's negative information getting on your credit report. If the bad information on your report looks completely foreign to you, contact the credit bureau (by phone or online) and explain that you need more information because you don't recognize the creditor.
- **If the creditor made a mistake:** Creditors make mistakes, too. You need to write or call the creditor to get it to correct the erroneous information that it sent to the credit bureau. Phoning the creditor first usually works best. (The credit bureau should be able to tell you how to reach the creditor if you don't know how.) If necessary, follow up with a letter or email to document and provide a record of your request.

TIP

Whether you speak with a credit bureau or an actual lender, make note of your conversations. If representatives say that they can fix the problem, get their names, email addresses, and phone extensions, and follow up with them if they don't deliver as promised. If you're ensnared in bureaucratic red tape, escalate the situation by speaking with a department manager. By law, bureaus are required to respond to a request to fix a credit error within 30 days — hold the bureau accountable! If they don't, you can submit a complaint to the Consumer Financial Protection Bureau at www.consumerfinance.gov/complaint or by calling 855-411-2372.

# Getting Your Credit Score

Many folks are disappointed to find that their credit reports lack their credit score. The reason for this is quite simple: The 2003 federal law mandating that the three credit agencies provide a free credit report annually to each U.S. citizen who requests a copy did *not* mandate that they provide the credit score. Thus, if you want to obtain your credit score, it's generally going to cost you.

One circumstance allows you to get one of your credit scores for free, but unfortunately, you can only do so when you're turned down for a loan. Current law allows you to obtain a free copy of the credit score a lender used in making a negative decision regarding your desired loan.

TIP

The credit score most lenders use today was developed by Fair Isaac Corporation and is called a *FICO score*. You can request your credit score from FICO, but you'll be charged $19.95 for every request (that can set you back about $60 to see your FICO score for all three credit bureaus). Save your money. In fact, you can get your current credit score without paying anything. You can start with the FICO score simulator at `www.myfico.com/free-credit-score-range-estimator`, which provides you with an estimated range for your FICO score based upon your answers to a short list of questions about your history with and usage of credit.

WARNING

If you do choose to pay for your current credit score, be crystal clear about what you're buying. You may not realize that you're agreeing to some sort of ongoing credit monitoring service for $100+ per year, an expenditure I don't generally feel is worthwhile.

## Interpreting your credit score

Your *credit score*, which is not the same as your credit report, is a three-digit score based on the report. Lenders use your credit score as a predictor of your likelihood of defaulting on repaying your borrowings. As such, your credit score has a major impact on whether a lender is willing to extend you a particular loan and at what interest rate.

FICO is the leading credit score in the industry. FICO scores range from a low of 300 to a high of 850. Most scores fall in the 600s and 700s. As with college entrance examinations, higher scores are better. (In recent years, the major credit bureaus — Equifax, Experian, and TransUnion — have developed their own credit scoring systems, but many lenders still use FICO the most.)

The higher your credit score, the lower your predicted likelihood of defaulting on a loan (see Figure 6-1). The "rate of credit delinquency" refers to the percentage of consumers who will become 90 days late or later in repaying a creditor within the next two years. As you can see in the chart, consumers with low credit scores have dramatically higher rates of falling behind on their loans. Thus, low credit scorers are considered much riskier borrowers, and fewer lenders are willing to offer them a given loan; those who do offer loans charge relatively high interest rates.

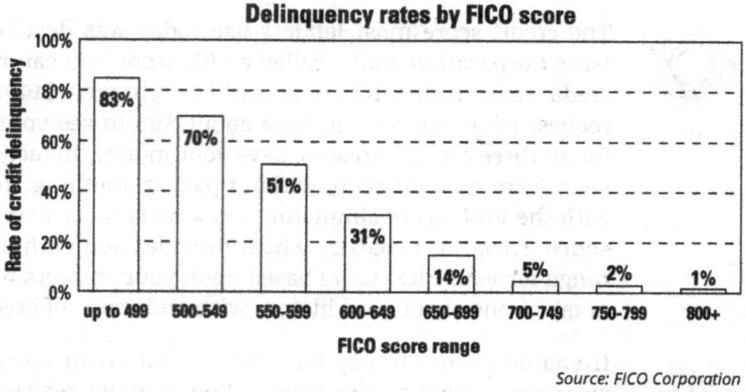


**FIGURE 6-1:** Lenders use credit scores to estimate how likely people are to default on a loan.

The median FICO score is around 720. You generally qualify for the best lending rates if your credit score is in the mid-700s or higher.

Your score can change whenever your credit report changes. But your score probably won't change a lot from one month to the next unless the information in your credit report changes substantially.

TIP

FICO makes the FICO scores as consistent as possible among the three credit-reporting agencies. But sometimes your FICO score may be quite different at each of the three credit-reporting agencies. Because lenders may review your score and credit report from any one of the three credit-reporting agencies, check your credit report at all three to make sure each is correct (see the earlier section "Obtaining your credit reports" to find out how to do that).

## Understanding how your FICO score is calculated

For a FICO score to be calculated from your credit report, the report must contain at least one account that has been open for six months or longer. In addition, the report must contain at least one account that has been updated in the past six months. This ensures that enough recent information is in your report to calculate a score.

The FICO score evaluates several categories of information: your payment history, the amount you owe, the length of your credit history, new credit you've acquired, types of credit you have in use, and the number of credit queries. Some, as you'd expect, are more important than others. It's important to note that

- **A score considers all these categories of information, not just one or two.** No one piece of information or factor alone determines your score.
- **The importance of any factor depends on the overall information in your credit report.** A given factor may be more important for some people than for others who have a different credit history. In addition, as the information in your credit report changes, so does the importance of any factor in determining your score. That's why it's impossible to say exactly how important any single factor is in determining your score — even the levels of importance shown in the following sections are for the general population and differ for different credit profiles.
- **Your FICO score looks only at information in your credit report.** Lenders often also look at other things when making a credit decision, including your income, how long you've worked at your present job, and the kind of credit you're requesting.
- **Your score considers both positive and negative information in your credit report.** Late payments lower your score, but establishing or reestablishing a good track record of making payments on time raises your score.
- **Raising your score is a bit like getting in shape.** It takes time, and there is no quick fix. In fact, quick-fix efforts can backfire. The best advice is to manage credit responsibly over time. The next section, "Improving your FICO score," provides some tips to get you started.

## Improving your FICO score

TIP

Here are some tips that can help improve your FICO score:

- **Have credit cards, but manage them responsibly.** In general, having credit cards and installment loans (and making timely payments) raises your score.
- **Keep balances low on credit cards and other revolving credit.** High outstanding debt can adversely affect a score.
- **Pay off debt.** The most effective way to improve your score in this area is by paying down your revolving credit.
- **Don't close unused credit cards as a short-term strategy to raise your score.** Generally, this doesn't work. In fact, it may *lower* your score. Late payments associated with old accounts won't disappear from your credit report if you close the account. Long-established accounts show that you have a longer history of managing credit, which is a good thing. And having available credit that you don't use doesn't lower your score. You may have reasons other than your score to shut down old credit card accounts that you don't use, but don't do it in hopes of getting a better score.
- **Don't open new credit card accounts that you don't need just to increase your available credit.** This approach can backfire and actually lower your score.

REMEMBER

Although a bankruptcy or late payment can quickly lower your score, improving your score takes time. If you're planning to apply for a mortgage, for example, it's a good idea to check your score (especially if you have reason to be concerned about your credit history) at least six months beforehand. That gives you time to take corrective action if needed. If you're actively working to improve your score, you should check it quarterly or even monthly to review changes.

## Tracking credit inquiries

A search for new credit can mean greater credit risk. This is why the FICO score counts inquiries — those requests a lender makes for your credit report or score when you apply for credit.

FICO scores consider inquiries very carefully because not all inquiries are related to credit risk. You should note three things about credit inquiries:

- **Inquiries don't affect scores very much.** For most people, one additional credit inquiry takes less than 5 points off their FICO score. However, inquiries can have a greater impact if you have few accounts or a short credit history. Large numbers of inquiries also mean greater risk: People with six inquiries or more on their credit reports are eight times more likely to declare bankruptcy than people with no inquiries on their reports.
- **Many kinds of inquiries aren't counted at all.** The score doesn't count it when you order your credit report or credit score from a credit-reporting agency. Also, the score doesn't count requests lenders make for your credit report or score in order to make you a preapproved credit offer or to review your account with them, even though you may see these inquiries on your credit report. Requests that are marked as coming from employers aren't counted either.
- **The score looks for *rate shopping*.** Looking for a mortgage or an auto loan may cause multiple lenders to request your credit report, even though you're looking for only one loan. To compensate for this, the score counts multiple inquiries in any 45-day period as just one inquiry. In addition, the score ignores *all* inquiries made in the 30 days prior to scoring. So if you find a loan within 30 days, the inquiries won't affect your score while you're rate shopping.

## What FICO scores ignore

**FICO scores consider a wide range of information on your credit report. However, they don't consider**

- Your race, color, religion, national origin, sex, or marital status.
- Any receipt of public assistance or the exercise of any consumer right (per U.S. law under the Consumer Credit Protection Act).
- Your age.
- Your salary, occupation, title, employer, date employed, or employment history.

## Gaining insight from rejections

When a lender receives your FICO score, up to four *score reasons* are also delivered. These are the top reasons why your score wasn't higher. If the lender rejects your request for credit and your FICO score was part of the reason, these score reasons can help the lender tell you why.

These score reasons can be more useful to you than the score itself. They help you determine whether your credit report may contain errors and how you may improve your credit score. However, if you already have a high FICO score (for example, in the mid-700s or higher), some of the reasons may not be as helpful, because they may be marginal factors related to less important categories, such as your length of credit history, new credit, and types of credit in use.

REMEMBER

No score, no matter how high or low, says whether you'll be a "good" or "bad" customer. Although many lenders use FICO scores to help them make lending decisions, each lender also has its own strategy, including the level of risk it finds acceptable for a given type of loan. There is no single minimum score used by all lenders.

# Boosting Your Credit Rating

Instead of simply throwing money into buying your credit scores or paying for some ongoing monitoring service to which you may not give much attention, take an interest in improving your credit standing and score. Working to boost your credit rating is especially worthwhile if you know that your credit report contains detrimental information.

Here are the most important actions that you can take to boost your attractiveness to lenders:

- **Get all three of your credit reports and be sure each is accurate.** Correct errors and be especially sure to get accounts removed from your credit report if they aren't yours and show late payments or are in collection.

- **Ask to have any late or missed payments that are more than seven years old removed.** Ditto for a bankruptcy that occurred more than ten years ago.
- **Pay all your bills on time.** To ensure on-time payments, sign up for automatic bill payment, a service that most companies (like phone and utility providers) offer.
- **Be loyal if it doesn't cost you.** The older your open loan accounts are, the better your credit rating will be. Closing old accounts and opening a bunch of new ones generally lowers your credit score. But don't be loyal if it costs you! For example, if you can refinance your mortgage and save some money, by all means do so. The same logic applies if you're carrying credit card debt at a high interest rate and want to transfer that balance to a lower-rate card. If your current credit card provider refuses to match a lower rate you find elsewhere, move your balance and save yourself some money.
- **Limit your debt and debt accounts.** The more loans, especially consumer loans, that you hold and the higher the balances, the lower your credit score will be. That said, your credit score will generally be maximized if you aren't using more than about 30 percent of your credit limits.
- **Work to pay down consumer revolving debt (such as credit card debt).** Turn to Chapter 4 for suggestions.

IN THIS CHAPTER

- » Prioritizing financial goals
- » Buying a car
- » Owning your home
- » Educating the kids
- » Planning your retirement

# Chapter 7 Financial Goals and Dreams

This chapter discusses the most common financial goals and how to work toward them. Naturally, you may have goals that are unique to your own situation. Accomplishing any such goals, however, almost always requires saving money. As one of my favorite proverbs says, "Do not wait until you are thirsty to dig a well," so don't wait to save money until you're ready to accomplish a personal or financial goal!

## Setting Financial Goals

The folks who accomplish their goals aren't necessarily smarter or higher-income earners than those who don't. People who identify their goals and then work toward them, which often requires changing some habits, are the ones who accomplish their goals. By understanding the basics of financial literacy and applying this knowledge to your situation, you will be better able to prioritize your financial goals and understand which habits you need to change to achieve those goals.

If you're accumulating money for a down payment on a home or to start or buy a business, for example, you'll probably need to save that money outside of a retirement account. Why? Because if you withdraw funds from retirement accounts before age 59½, not only do you have to pay income taxes on the withdrawals, but you also generally have to pay *early withdrawal penalties* of 10 percent of the withdrawn amount in federal tax plus whatever your state charges. Retirement accounts shelter your money from taxation, but some financial goals are not easily achieved by saving in retirement accounts. Also, retirement accounts have caps on the amount you can contribute annually.

TIP

Learn how to delay or modify gratification. Get into the habit of saving for your larger consumer purchases to avoid paying for them over time with high-interest consumer credit. When saving up for a consumer purchase such as a car, a money-market account or short-term bond fund (see Chapter 5) is a good place to store your short-term savings.

## Saving on a Car

The following are some tips and strategies for making the most of your car-driving experiences and doing so in a financially prudent fashion:

- **Don't buy a car in the first place.** Car ownership is costly. As a result, I suggest that if you don't need a car, don't buy one — particularly if you live in a city with reliable public transportation or you rarely need a car. Use the subway or bus and save your money. Enjoy the times when you can do without a car because you may save a good deal of money and hassle.
- **Pay cash.** Shun leasing and borrowing. When you do decide to get your own car, do your best to save in advance and pay for the car with your cash savings. For many folks starting out, doing so means setting their sights on a quality used car.

  WARNING

  Taking out a loan to buy a car or leasing a car are generally much-more-expensive ways to get a car because of the interest you pay (in the case of a loan) or the higher rates (in the case of leasing). Car dealers who are in the business of leasing or originating car loans will, of course, have a different agenda and push these methods because they profit from them. Don't be fooled by zero percent interest loans, either — dealers will sock you with a higher car price to make up for such low-cost financing.

» **Consider total costs:** When you compare makes and models of cars, be sure to consider more than the sticker price. Among other cost considerations are fuel, maintenance, repairs, insurance, and how rapidly the car depreciates in value. Among the best independent sources that I've found for such information are `www.edmunds.com/tco.html` and `www.motortrend.com/intellichoice`.

» **Compare new with used:** Because a new car depreciates most rapidly in value in the first couple of years, buying a car that's at least a year or two old usually provides you with a better value for your money than buying a new car.

REMEMBER

Don't assume, however, that buying a used car is always a better value. For example, during a severe recession such as the one the United States experienced in 2008–2009, new cars made comparatively better sense than many used cars. The reason for this was a matter of simple economics and supply and demand. More people opted for buying a used car. Fewer folks put theirs on the market, holding off on buying a new one until the economy got better. These two forces squeezed used-car supply and increased used-car prices. At the same time, fewer consumers were buying new cars, forcing dealers to slash new-car prices.

» **Understand a car's real value before negotiating:** Be sure to do some basic research regarding the pricing of the car type you desire to assist you as you shop around. For new cars, you should know (and can easily find out) what the dealer's cost is for each vehicle. You can find this information at *Consumer Reports* (`www.consumerreports.org`) as well as the sources I mention in the next paragraph.

For used cars, a number of sources can assist you with quickly valuing a vehicle based on its condition, features, and mileage. Among the best sources for used-car valuation information are Kelley Blue Book (`www.kbb.com`) and Edmunds (`www.edmunds.com`).

# Saving for a Home

*Before* you set out in search of your dream home, one of the single most important questions you should answer is, "What can I afford to spend on a home?" To answer that question intelligently, you first need to understand what your financial goals are, what it will take to achieve them, and where you are today.

The following sections explain the basics of how mortgages work, and describe other expenses of buying and owning a home that you must budget for. Be sure that you consider all these expenses — not just your mortgage payment — when you save for a home.

## Understanding mortgage essentials

A *mortgage* is a loan you take out to buy a home. A mortgage allows you to purchase a $200,000 home even though you have far less money than that to put toward the purchase. Almost all mortgages require monthly payments over a 15- or 30-year time span. Almost always, the largest component of housing costs is your mortgage.

Here's basically how a mortgage works. Suppose that you're purchasing a $300,000 home and that you have diligently saved a 20 percent ($60,000, in this example) down payment. Thus, you're in the market for a $240,000 mortgage loan.

Beyond your down payment, the size of your monthly mortgage payment is affected by other factors, such as interest rates and your credit rating, and whether you choose a 15- or 30-year time span to repay the loan.

When you sit down with a mortgage lender, they ask you to complete a volume of paperwork that dwarfs what's required for your annual income tax return. Then the lender proceeds to give you an even bigger headache by talking about the literally hundreds of mortgage permutations and options. You can read more about these many details in the most recent edition of my book *Home Buying Kit For Dummies* (Wiley).

REMEMBER

Just because a lender or real estate agent says you're eligible for, or can qualify for, a certain size loan doesn't mean that's what you can afford given your personal financial situation. Lenders *can't* tell you what you can afford — they can tell you *only* the maximum that they'll lend to you. Ultimately, a lender doesn't care about you, your financial situation, or your other needs as long as it has protected its financial interests. This is true whether you're borrowing to buy a car or a home.

Calculating the size of your mortgage payment, after you know the amount you want to borrow, is simple. The hard part for most people is determining how much they can afford to borrow, as you are usually on your own to account for the other expenses of owning a home. The next section helps you identify and estimate these expenses.

## Budgeting for monthly expenses

Determining the exact amount of mortgage that allows you to stay within the boundaries of what you can afford is a little challenging, because the housing cost you figure that you can afford is made up of several components, including

- **Mortgage payments:** This is typically the biggest component of your housing expense.
- **Property taxes:** As a homeowner, you must pay property taxes to your local government (unless you live in a state without property taxes). Property taxes are typically based on the value of a property. Although an average property tax rate is about 1.5 to 2.0 percent of the property's value per year, you should understand what the exact rate is in your area. Call the tax collector's office in the town where you're contemplating buying a home and ask what the property tax rate is and what additional fees and assessments may apply.

  WARNING

  Don't rely on property tax information included in real-estate listings, which can be outdated.
- **Insurance:** Your mortgage lender almost surely won't allow you to close the purchase until you demonstrate that you have proper homeowner's insurance. If you buy the home and make a down payment of, say, 20 percent of the purchase price, the lender is putting up the other 80 percent of the purchase price. So if the home burns to the ground and is a total loss, the lender has more invested financially than you do. In most states, your home is the lender's security for the loan.

TIP

When you purchase homeowner's insurance, you should buy the most comprehensive coverage that you can and take the highest deductible that you can afford to help minimize the cost.

» **Maintenance:** Although lenders don't care about maintenance expenses in figuring what you can afford to buy, you shouldn't overlook this significant expense. As a rule of thumb, expect to spend about 1 percent of your home's purchase price each year on maintenance.

  With some types of housing, such as condominiums, you actually pay monthly dues into a homeowners' association, which takes care of the maintenance for the complex. In that case, you're responsible for maintaining only the interior of your unit. Before you buy such a unit, check with the association to see what the dues are, what funds they currently have in hand for future capital repairs or replacements per their reserve study, and whether any new special assessments are planned or likely for unfunded deficient conditions.

» **Nonessential home improvements:** Be aware (and beware) of what you may spend on nonessential home improvements. This *Other* category can really get you into trouble. Advertisements, your neighbors, and your co-workers can all entice you into blowing big bucks on new furniture, endless remodeling projects, landscaping — you name it.

REMEMBER

Budget for these nonessentials; otherwise, your home can become a money pit by causing you to spend too much, not save enough, and (possibly) go into debt via credit/debit cards and the like.

## Grasping the tax benefits of homeownership

One of the benefits of homeownership is that the IRS and most state governments allow you to deduct, within certain limits, mortgage interest and property taxes when you file your annual income tax return.

Just because mortgage interest and property taxes are allowable deductions on your income tax return, don't think that the government is literally paying for these items for you. Consider that when you earn a dollar of income and must pay income tax on that dollar, you don't pay the entire dollar back to the government in taxes. Your tax bracket (see Chapter 9) determines the amount of taxes you pay on that dollar.

Here's a shortcut that works reasonably well in determining your tax savings in homeownership: Multiply your federal tax rate by the portion of your property taxes up to $10,000 when combined with your annual state income tax payments, and the portion of your mortgage payment on up to $750,000 of mortgage debt.

TIP

Even if you're under the $750,000 threshold, not all of your mortgage payment is tax-deductible — only the portion of the mortgage payment that goes toward interest. Technically, you pay federal and state taxes, so you should consider your state tax savings as well when calculating your homeownership tax savings. However, to keep things simple and still get a reliable estimate, simply multiply your mortgage payment and property taxes by your *federal* income tax rate. This shortcut works well because the small portion of your mortgage payment that isn't deductible (because it's for the loan repayment) approximately offsets the overlooked state tax savings.

If you want to more accurately determine how homeownership may affect your tax situation, get out your tax return and try plugging in some reasonable numbers to estimate how your taxes will change. You can also speak with a tax advisor. As for what future tax changes may occur, I don't expect anything dramatic. There has been some talk of raising the $10,000 cap in property and state income tax deductions, which would be a small win for home buyers and owners.

TIP

Use the following table to calculate your monthly expenses for owning a home. Notice that you must budget for many components beyond your mortgage payment.

| Item | Estimated Monthly Expense |
| --- | --- |
| Mortgage payment | $ |
| Property taxes | +$ |
| Insurance | +$ |
| Improvements and maintenance | +$ |

| Item | Estimated Monthly Expense |
| --- | --- |
| Homeownership expenses | =$ |
| Tax savings | –$ |
| Homeownership expenses (after tax savings) | =$ |

## Considering closing costs

On the day when a home becomes yours officially, known as *closing day*, many people (in addition to the seller) will have their hands in your wallet. Myriad one-time closing costs can leave you poorer or send you running to your relatives for financial assistance. In a typical real-estate deal, closing costs total 2 to 5 percent of the property's purchase price. Thus, you shouldn't ignore them in figuring the amount of money you need to close the deal. Having enough to pay the down payment on your loan isn't sufficient.

## Accumulating the down payment

Ideally, when buying a home you should have enough money accumulated for a down payment of 20 percent of the property's purchase price. Twenty percent down is generally a big enough cushion to protect lenders from losing money if you default on the loan.

Almost all mortgage lenders require you to obtain (and pay for) private mortgage insurance (PMI) if your down payment is less than 20 percent of the property's purchase price. Depending on the price of the home you buy, PMI can add from several hundred to a thousand dollars or more annually to your loan's cost.

When you make a down payment of less than 20 percent, you can also expect worse loan terms, such as higher up-front fees and/or a higher ongoing interest rate on a mortgage.

REMEMBER

PMI isn't a permanent cost. Your need for PMI vanishes when you can prove that you have at least 20 percent *equity* (home value minus loan balance outstanding) in the property. The 20 percent can come from loan paydown, appreciation, improvements that enhance the property's value, or any combination thereof. Note also that to remove PMI, most mortgage lenders require that an appraisal be done — at your expense.

## Where to invest the down payment

As with all informed investing decisions, which investment(s) you consider for money earmarked for your down payment should be determined by how soon you need the money back. The longer the time frame during which you can invest, the more growth-oriented and riskier (that is, more *volatile*) an investment you may consider. Conversely, when you have a short time frame — five years or less — during which you can invest, choosing volatile investments is dangerous.

WARNING

When the stock market is rising, some folks are tempted to keep down-payment money in stocks. Investing down-payment money in stocks is a dangerous strategy. Your expected home purchase may be delayed for years due to a sinking investment portfolio. Stocks are a generally inappropriate investment for down-payment money you expect to tap within the next five years. More aggressive individual stocks should have an even longer time horizon — ideally, seven to ten or more years.

## Investments for five years or less

The sooner you expect to buy, the less risk you should take. Although it may appear boring, the first (and likely best) place for accumulating your down-payment money is in a money market mutual fund. When you invest in these funds, the value of your original investment (principal) doesn't fluctuate. Rather, you simply earn interest on the money that you've invested. Money market funds invest in super-safe investments, such as Treasury bills, bank certificates of deposit, and *commercial paper* (short-term IOUs issued by the most creditworthy corporations).

TIP

When choosing a money market fund in which to invest, considering your tax status may be helpful in maximizing your earnings. For more on how this works and some specific fund recommendations, see the latest edition of my book *Mutual Funds For Dummies* (Wiley).

## Investments for more than five years

Should you expect to hold onto your home-down-payment money for more than five years, you can comfortably consider riskier investments, such as longer-term bonds, as well as more conservative stocks. See Chapter 5 for more about these and other investment vehicles.

## Ways to buy with less money down

If saving a 20 percent down payment plus closing costs seems like an insurmountable mountain given your personal financial situation, don't panic, and don't give up! Here's a grab bag filled with time-tested ways to overcome this seemingly gargantuan obstacle:

- **Boost your savings rate:** Being efficient with your spending is always a good financial habit, but saving faster is a *necessity* for nearly all prospective home buyers. Most people have fat in their budgets. Start by reading Chapter 2 for ways to assess your current spending and boost your savings rate.
- **Set your sights lower.** Twenty percent of a big number is a big number, so it stands to reason that 20 percent of a smaller number is a smaller number. If the down payment and closing costs needed to purchase a $300,000 home are stretching you, scale back to a $240,000 or $200,000 home, which should slash your required cash for the home purchase by about 20 to 33 percent.
- **Check out low-down-payment loan programs.** Some lenders offer low-down-payment mortgage programs, typically in exchange for higher interest rates and the purchase of private mortgage insurance (PMI). The best low-down-payment loan is the FHA purchase program, which requires a down payment of only 3.5 percent with a credit rating of 580 or higher (see `www.fhaloans.com`). If you are a veteran, look into getting a VA loan.

  Another way to buy a home with no down payment and a low interest rate in "rural" areas is via the USDA's Single Family Housing Guaranteed Loan Program (`www.rd.usda.gov/programs-services/single-family-housing-guaranteed-loan-program`). These properties are not limited to what one would typically think of as "rural" areas (think more broadly about non-urban areas) and while there are income limits, many folks qualify.

TIP

Unless you're chomping at the bit to purchase a home, take more time and try to accumulate a larger down payment. However, if you're the type of person who has trouble saving and may never save a 20 percent down payment, buying with less money down may be your best option. In this situation, be sure to shop around for the best loan terms.

- **Access retirement accounts.** Some employers allow you to borrow against your retirement savings plan. Just be sure that you understand the repayment rules so you don't get tripped up and forced to treat the withdrawal as a taxable distribution. You're allowed to make penalty-free withdrawals from Individual Retirement Accounts for a first-time home purchase.
- **Get family help.** Your folks or grandparents may like, perhaps even love, to help you with the down payment and closing costs for your dream home. If they have substantial assets, holding onto all these assets until their death may trigger estate or inheritance taxes. Or maybe they're bank-and-bond-type investors and are earning paltry returns.
- **Look into seller financing.** Some sellers don't need all the cash from the sale of their property when the transaction closes escrow. These sellers may be willing to offer you a second mortgage to help you buy their property. In fact, they often advertise that they're willing to assist with financing. Seller financing is usually due and payable in five to ten years. This gives you time to build up equity or save enough to refinance into a new, larger, 80 percent conventional mortgage before the seller's loan comes due.

  WARNING

  Be cautious about seller financing. Some sellers who offer property with built-in financing are trying to dump a house that has major defects. It's also possible that the house may be priced far above its fair market value. Before accepting seller financing, make sure that the property doesn't have fatal flaws (have a thorough inspection conducted) and is priced competitively. Also be sure that the seller financing interest rate is as low as or lower than the rate you can obtain through a traditional mortgage lender.
- **Get partners.** With many things in life, there is strength in numbers. You may be able to get more home for your money and may need to come up with less up-front cash if you find partners for a multiunit real estate purchase. For example, you can find one or two other partners and go in together to purchase a duplex or triplex.

WARNING

Before you go into a partnership to buy a building, be sure to consider all the "what ifs." What if one of you wants out after a year? What if one of you fails to pay the pro-rata share of expenses? What if one of you wants to remodel and the other doesn't? And so forth. Have a lawyer prepare a co-ownership agreement that explicitly delineates how issues like these will be dealt with. Otherwise, you can face some major disagreements down the road, even if you go in together with friends or people you think you know well.

# Planning for College Costs

How you help pay for your child's college costs depends on your own unique situation and personal philosophy. However, in most cases, you may have to borrow some money, even if you have some available cash that can be directed to pay the college bills as you receive them.

TIP

Ask yourself what the best way is to help pay for college and what you want/expect in the way of contributions by your children. Even parents who can afford to pay the entire costs often require their children to contribute something meaningful in terms of costs — whether from savings over summer work, loans, and so on.

## Setting realistic savings goals

If you have money left over after taking advantage of retirement accounts, by all means, try to save for your children's college costs. You should save in your name unless you know you aren't going to apply for financial aid.

Be realistic about what you can afford for college expenses given your other financial goals, especially saving for retirement. If you're not a high-income earner, consider trying to save enough to pay a third or, at most, half of the cost. You can make up the balance through loans, your child's employment before and during college, and the like.

Use Table 7-1 to help get a handle on how much you should be saving for college. I've kept this table simple, and it ignores the growth in your investment balances over time. If you'd like to use an online calculator, try Vanguard's at `https://vanguardcollege.ssnc.cloud/collcost.php`.

**TABLE 7-1 How Much to Save for College**

| Figure Out This | Write It Here |
|---|---|
| 1. *Four-year total cost of the school you think your child will attend | $ ______________ |
| 2. Percent of costs you'd like to pay (for example, 20% or 40%) | × ______________% |
| 3. Line 1 times Line 2 (the amount you'll pay in today's dollars) | = $ ______________ |
| 4. Number of months until your child reaches college age | ÷ ____________ months |
| 5. **Line 3 divided by Line 4 (amount to save per month in today's dollars) | = $ __________ / month |

**The average cost of a four-year private college education today is about $220,000; the average cost of a four-year public college education is about $108,000. If your child has an expensive taste in schools, you may want to tack 20 to 30 percent onto the average figures.*

***The amount you need to save (calculated in Line 5) "in today's dollars" does need to be increased once per year to reflect the increase in college inflation – 3 or 4 percent should do.*

## Understanding the expected family contribution

The financial aid process and associated forms at colleges and universities collect a lot of information and data. The Free Application for Federal Student Aid (FAFSA) uses a federal formula to determine the so-called *expected family contribution* (EFC). This is the amount that the family can supposedly afford to pay annually toward their child's college costs.

The federal formula for determining the EFC considers parental income (outside of retirement accounts) and family assets (such as equity in real estate and business that you own). Financial aid officers can also tweak numbers based upon how badly they want your child, or if they feel that there are extenuating circumstances.

TIP

Although the federal financial aid analysis no longer counts equity in your primary residence as an asset, many private (independent) schools ask parents for this information when making their own financial aid determinations. Therefore, depending on where your child goes to college, paying down your home mortgage more quickly instead of funding retirement accounts can harm you financially: You may end up with less financial aid and a higher tax bill.

## Finding financial aid and other resources

The expected family contribution (EFC) is compared with and subtracted from the college's total cost of attendance — which includes tuition, room, board, books, travel, and personal expenses. If the EFC is equal to or greater than the school's cost of attendance, a family shouldn't expect any reduction in price through need-based financial aid. The family could still possibly receive a price reduction through merit scholarships.

In many cases, however, the total cost of attendance at a given college exceeds a family's EFC. The difference can be made up with grants and scholarships, federal work-study, and student loans.

TIP

If you're a homeowner, you may be able to borrow against the *equity* (market value minus the outstanding mortgage loan) in your property. This option is useful because you can borrow against your home at a reasonable interest rate, and the interest is generally tax-deductible subject to IRS limits (typically on up to $750,000 of mortgage debt). Some company retirement plans — for example, 401(k)s — allow borrowing as well.

WARNING

Parents are allowed to make penalty-free withdrawals from individual retirement accounts if the funds are used for college expenses. Although you won't be charged an early-withdrawal penalty, the IRS (and most states) will treat the amount withdrawn as taxable income. On top of that, the financial aid office will look at your beefed-up income and assume that you don't need as much financial aid. Because of these negative ramifications, funding college costs in this fashion should only be done as an absolute last resort.

Check out the latest edition of my book *Paying For College For Dummies* (Wiley) for all the details on higher education alternatives and how to best afford them.

## Saving and investing: Long-term strategies

Saving is a good thing to do, but there are better and worse ways to do so from the perspective of how colleges set their pricing/ financial aid awards. You may think that money is money, but the financial aid system doesn't treat all money, saving, and investments equally — not even close!

### Financial aid treatment of retirement accounts

Under the current financial aid needs analysis system, the value of your retirement plans is not considered an asset. By contrast, money that you save outside retirement accounts, especially money in the child's name, is counted as an asset and reduces financial aid eligibility and increases the price colleges will charge you.

### Financial aid treatment of money in the kids' names

If you plan to apply for financial aid, save money in your name rather than in your children's names (such as via custodial accounts). Colleges expect a much greater percentage of the money in your children's names (20 percent) to be used annually for college costs than the money in your name (about 5.65 percent).

However, if you're affluent enough to foot your child's college bill without outside help, investing in your kid's name can potentially save you a little money in taxes. One way to do this is with custodial accounts. Parents control a custodial account until the child reaches either the age of 18 or 21, depending upon the state in which you reside. Upon reaching age 18 (or age 24 if your offspring are still full-time students), all income generated by investments in your child's name is taxed at your child's rate, which is presumably a lower tax rate than yours.

### 529 state-sponsored college savings plans

The 529 plans (named after Internal Revenue Code Section 529 and also known as qualified state tuition plans) are educational savings plans. A parent or grandparent can generally put more than $300,000 per beneficiary into one of these plans.

These plans have both pros and cons. They generally make the most sense for higher income parents who don't expect their children to qualify for financial aid. However, less affluent parents may want to consider saving some money in these plans as the investment returns aren't taxed when the money is used for educational expenses. Grandparents can consider such plans as well.

REMEMBER

Do a lot of research and homework before investing in any plan. Check out the investment track record, allocations, and fees of each plan, as well as restrictions on transferring to other plans or changing beneficiaries.

Please also be aware that a future Congress could change the tax laws affecting these plans, diminishing the tax breaks or increasing the penalties for nonqualified withdrawals.

### Investing strategies and vehicles

Low-cost mutual funds and exchange-traded funds (ETFs) are excellent investment vehicles when investing. When investing for a long-term goal like your retirement, which may be decades in the future, investing mostly or completely in stock-focused funds makes sense.

In my book *Investing For Dummies* (Wiley), in addition to stocks, I also discuss how to invest in real estate and small business to build wealth over the long term. If you build equity in investment real-estate properties or in a small business, you may be able to pay for college expenses in the future by using some of those investments' cash flow or by borrowing against the equity of those assets.

Lending type investments, which include things like bank accounts and bonds, tend to produce lower long-term returns but are generally less volatile in value in the shorter term. Having a chunk of money in those types of investments, especially as your child nears entering college, makes good financial sense.

## Saving strategies for late starters

If you're getting a late start saving for college costs, here are some examples of moves you may consider making:

- **Find sensible ways to reduce your taxable income.** All other things being equal, of course, you shouldn't simply accept less income, because you'll be better off generally with higher income. That said, there may be some sensible steps you can take to keep a lid on your taxable income, as doing so should help improve financial aid offers. For example, with your investments, you have some control over the timing of when you sell an investment at a profit and realize capital gains.

- **Remember that retirement account money is generally ignored by the financial aid process.** Keep in mind, however, that for the contributions made during the previous two years, reported on your financial aid forms, the financial aid analysis process will add those contributions back to your taxable income. So, be sure to contribute more if you can in the years prior to those base years.
- **Reduce your cash by making planned purchases.** If one of your cars needs replacing, you may want to do so before your kids apply to college and use up some of your cash for that purchase. You don't want to go overboard, of course, but the reduced cash should improve the pricing offers you get from colleges.
- **Pay off high-cost debt.** If you have debt outstanding on credit cards, auto loans, and the like and you have cash to pay it off, consider doing so. Again, the reduced cash can help improve your financial aid awards. And the financial aid needs analysis ignores and doesn't make any allowance for your consumer debt.
- **Use assets in kids' names.** If you put money into your kids' names in the past and now realize that wasn't a wise move, perhaps you have current expenses for their benefit that you can use some of this money for. One obvious example would be private K–12 schooling or travel sports teams. If you have kids, you don't need me to remind you of all the things you spend money on for them!

# Developing a Retirement Plan

**Most people have a long-term financial goal of retiring someday. For some, doing so means leaving paid work behind entirely. To others, simply cutting back on work or doing something completely different on a part-time basis is most appealing.**

If you don't plan to work well into your golden years, you need a reasonable amount of savings/investments, which includes monthly Social Security benefits, in order to maintain a particular lifestyle in the absence of your normal employment income. The following sections help you get started on determining how much money you need and coming to grips with those numbers.

REMEMBER

If you are married, be sure that you and your spouse coordinate your individual retirement plans when you begin retirement planning. Doing so may seem obvious, but it's an important step. Discussions about retirement plans need to begin long before retirement. Even when one spouse is doing most of the financial planning for retirement, both spouses need to have a meeting of the minds over the nonfinancial aspects of their senior years. And the spouse who is not doing as much of the financial planning still needs to know the overall financial situation.

## Figuring out what portion of income you need

If you're like most people, you need less money to live on in retirement than during your working years. That's because in retirement most people don't need to save any of their income and many of their work-related expenses (commuting, work clothes, and such) go away or greatly decrease. With less income, most retirees find that they pay less in taxes, too.

On the flip side, some categories of expenses may go up in retirement. With more free time on your hands, you may spend more on entertainment, restaurants, and travel. The costs for prescription drugs and other medical expenses also can begin to add up.

To help figure out how much money you need, keep the following statistics in mind. Studies have shown that retirees typically spend 65 to 80 percent of their pre-retirement income during their retirement years. Folks at the lower end of this range typically

- Save a large portion of their annual earnings during their working years
- Don't have a mortgage or any other debt in retirement
- Are higher-income earners who don't anticipate leading a lifestyle in retirement that's reflective of their current high income

Those who spend at the higher end of the range tend to have the following characteristics:

- » Save little or none of their annual earnings before retirement
- » Still have a significant mortgage or growing rent to pay in retirement
- » Need nearly all current income to meet their current lifestyle
- » Have expensive hobbies that they have more time to pursue

TIP

Numerous useful retirement planning analytic tools are available that you can use to assess where you currently stand in terms of saving for retirement. Among the various mass market website retirement tools, I really like T. Rowe Price's (www.troweprice.com/usis/advice/tools/retirement-income-calculator) and Vanguard's (investor.vanguard.com/calculator-tools/retirement-income-calculator/).

REMEMBER

I can't offer a definitive answer as to how much you personally may need to have for your retirement. Just make sure that you carefully look at all your expenses and figure out how they may change.

## Eyeing the components of your retirement plan

In order to meet your retirement goals, you need a firm grasp of which resources are available to help you. In addition to government benefits such as Social Security, company-provided pensions, and personal investments round out most people's retirement income sources. This section takes a closer look at these elements.

### Social Security retirement benefits

Social Security is intended to provide a subsistence/modest level of income in retirement for basic living necessities such as food, shelter, and clothing. However, Social Security wasn't designed to be a retiree's sole source of income. When planning for retirement, you'll likely need to supplement your expected Social Security benefits with personal savings, investments, and company pension benefits. If you're a high-income earner, you particularly need to supplement your income — unless, of course, you're willing to live well beneath your pre-retirement income.

If you're still working, you can estimate your Social Security retirement benefits by looking at your most recent Social Security benefits summary at www.ssa.gov/myaccount/ or by calling 800-772-1213 and requesting Form SSA-7004 ("Request for Social Security Statement"). Setting up a "my Social Security" account on the Social Security website lets you obtain updated benefits estimates, verify your earnings, and take other actions.

By reviewing your Social Security account, you can see how much in Social Security benefits you've already earned and review how the Social Security Administration (SSA) determines these numbers. With this information, you can better plan for your retirement and make important retirement planning decisions.

TIP

If you want to delve into different scenarios for your Social Security benefits, use the SSA's online Retirement Estimator at www.ssa.gov/benefits/retirement/estimator.html.

## Pensions

When putting together your retirement plan, you also want to consider any pensions you have available to you. Also known as a *defined benefit plan*, a company pension plan is one that your employer actually is contributing to and investing money in to fund your future pension payments.

If your current or previous employers have a pension plan and you may have accumulated benefits, request a copy of each plan's benefit description and a recent statement of your earned benefits. (When you crunch the numbers for your retirement plan, you need your pension benefit statements.)

Based on your years of service, your benefits statement will show you how much of a benefit you've earned. Your current employer's statement or the person or department that works with benefits may also be able to show you how your pension benefits will increase based on working until a certain future age.

## Investments

The many types of investments you may have are an important component of your retirement plan. These investments may come in various forms, such as bank accounts, brokerage accounts, mutual fund accounts, and so on. Your investments may or may not be in retirement accounts. Even if they aren't, they still can be earmarked to help with your retirement.

Take an inventory of your savings and investments by gathering recent copies of your statements (or checking balances online if you've gone paperless) from the following types of accounts or investment options:

- Bank accounts — checking (especially if they hold excess savings), savings, CDs, and so on
- IRA accounts
- Taxable accounts at brokers and mutual funds
- Employer retirement accounts, including
  - Profit-sharing plans
  - Employee stock ownership plans (ESOPs)
  - 401(k)s, 403(b)s, and so on
- Investment real estate

You will use this inventory of your current assets in the "Crunching the numbers" section to determine where you stand regarding retirement planning.

### Your home's equity

If you've owned a home over the years and it has a decent amount of *equity* in it (the difference between its market value and the mortgage debt owed on it), you can tap into that equity to provide for your retirement. In order to tap into your home's equity, you have two primary options:

- **You can sell your home.** After you sell your home, you can either buy a less costly one or rent.
- **You can take out a reverse mortgage.** With a *reverse mortgage,* you continue to live in your home and draw income against your home, which is accumulated as a debt balance to be paid once the home is sold.

If you're pretty certain you'd like to tap your home's equity to help with retirement, consider how much equity you would use.

## Crunching the numbers

Numerous mass market website tools exist and focus on retirement planning. Many investment firms offer these to lure you to their websites. Some require you to register whereas others can be accessed as a "guest." Such tools walk you through the calculations needed to figure out how much you should be saving to reach your retirement goal.

The assumptions that you plug into these calculators are really important, so here's a review of the key ones:

- **Asset allocation:** Enter your current *allocation* (the portion invested in stocks versus bonds). You'll also typically select an allocation for after you're retired. Most such calculators don't include real estate as a possible asset. If you own real estate as an investment, you should treat those assets as a stock-like investment, since they have similar long-term risk and return characteristics. (Calculate your equity in investment real estate, which is the difference between a property's current market value and mortgage debt on that property.)
- **Age of retirement:** Plug in your preferred age of retirement, within reason, of course. There's no point plugging in a dream number like "I'd like to retire by age 45, but I know the only way I can do that is to win the lottery!" Depending on how the analysis works out, you can always go back and plug in a different age.
- **Include Social Security:** Some calculators ask whether you want to include expected Social Security benefits. I'd rather that they didn't pose this question at all, because you definitely should include your Social Security benefits in the calculations. Based on your current income, the calculator will automatically plug in your estimated benefits. So long as your income hasn't changed or won't change dramatically, using the calculator's estimated number should be fine. Alternatively, you can use your personal information that you can access on the Social Security website at www.ssa.gov.

Many calculators allow you to make adjustments, such as to your desired age of retirement, rate of savings, and to what age you'd like your savings to last. So, for example, if the analysis shows that you have much more than enough to retire by age 65, try plugging in, say, age 62 and voilà, the calculator quickly shows you how the numbers change.

TIP

Among the mass market website retirement planning tools and booklets, I like T. Rowe Price's. Visit www.troweprice.com for the online version or call 800-638-5660 for the work booklets. The T. Rowe Price web-based Retirement Income Calculator (www.troweprice.com/usis/advice/tools/retirement-income-calculator) is a user-friendly tool, and the website says it takes about 10 minutes to complete. If you're organized and have your documents handy, you may cruise through it quickly, but otherwise you'll more than likely need 20 to 30 minutes.

## Making the numbers work

After you crunch the numbers, you may discover that you need to save at a rate that isn't doable. Don't despair. You have the following options to lessen the depressingly high savings you apparently need:

- **Boost your investment returns.** Reduce your taxes while investing: While you're still working, be sure to take advantage of retirement savings accounts, especially when you can gain free matching money from your employer or you're eligible for the special tax credit from the government. When investing money outside of retirement accounts, take care to minimize taxes. For more on investing strategies, see Chapter 5.
- **Work (a little) more.** Extend the number of years you're willing to work or consider working part time for a few years past the age you were expecting to stop working.
- **Reduce your spending.** The more you spend today, the more years you'll have to work in order to meet your savings goal.
- **Use your home's equity.** If you didn't factor using some of your home's equity into your retirement nest egg, consider doing so. Some people are willing to trade down into a less costly property in retirement. You also can take a reverse mortgage to tap some of your current home's equity. See the earlier section "Your home's equity."

## Dealing with excess money

If you find yourself with extra money, the good news is that you can have peace of mind and more confidence about achieving your desired standard of living during retirement. In this situation, consider taking either of the following actions:

- **Enhance your retirement.** Don't be afraid to enjoy yourself. While you're still healthy, travel, eat out, take some classes, and do whatever else floats your boat (within reason, of course). Remember that come the end of your life, you can't take your money with you.
- **Earmark a portion of your assets for your beneficiaries.** You may want to leave something for your family members as well as other beneficiaries, such as your place of worship and charities. If so, you need to determine the approximate dollar amount for each of the beneficiaries.

REMEMBER

Of course, life can throw you unexpected curveballs that may cause you to incur higher-than-expected expenses. But if you're always preparing for rainy day after rainy day, you may lead a miserly, unenjoyable retirement.

## Investing in retirement accounts when you're young

During your younger adult years, you may not be thinking much about retirement because it seems to be well off in the distance. But if you'd like to scale back on your work schedule someday, partly or completely, you're best off saving toward that goal as soon as you start drawing a regular paycheck.

Where possible, try to save and invest in accounts that offer you a tax advantage, which is precisely what retirement accounts offer you. These accounts — known by such enlightening acronyms and names as 401(k), 403(b), SEP-IRA, and so on — offer tax breaks to people of all economic means. Consider the following advantages to investing in retirement accounts:

- **Contributions often provide up-front tax breaks.** By investing through a retirement account, you not only plan wisely for your future but also get an immediate financial reward: lower taxes, which mean more money available for saving and investing. Retirement account contributions generally aren't taxed at either the federal or state income tax level until withdrawal (but they're still subject to Social Security and Medicare taxes when earned). If you're paying, say, 30 percent between federal and state taxes, a $4,000 contribution to a retirement account lowers your income taxes by $1,200.

Modest income earners also may get an additional government tax credit known as the Retirement Savings Contributions Credit. A maximum credit of 50 percent applies to the first $2,000 contributed for single taxpayers with an adjusted gross income (AGI) of no more than $23,750, and married couples filing jointly with an AGI of $47,500 or less. Singles with an AGI of between $23,750 and $25,500 and married couples with an AGI between $47,500 and $51,000 are eligible for a 20 percent tax credit. Single taxpayers with an AGI of more than $25,500 but no more than $39,500, as well as married couples with an AGI between $51,000 and $79,000, can get a 10 percent tax credit.

- **Your employer may match some of your contributions.** This cash is free money from your employer, and it's use it or lose it, so don't miss out!
- **Investment returns compound tax-free.** After you put money into a retirement account, you get to defer taxes on all the accumulating gains and profits (including interest and dividends) until you withdraw the money down the road. Thus, more money is working for you over a longer period of time. (One exception: Roth IRAs offer no up-front tax breaks but permit tax-free withdrawal of investment earnings in retirement.)

## Surveying retirement account choices

A *retirement account* is simply a shell or shield that keeps the federal, state, and local governments from taxing your investment earnings each year. You choose which investments you want to hold inside your retirement account shell.

If you earn employment income (or receive alimony), you have options for putting money away in a retirement account that compounds without taxation until you withdraw the money. In most cases, your contributions to these retirement accounts are tax-deductible.

The following list describes the types of retirement accounts that are suited to various situations:

- **Company-based retirement plans:** Larger for-profit companies generally offer their employees a *401(k)* plan, which typically allows saving up to $23,500 per year (for tax year 2025). Many nonprofit organizations offer their employees similar plans, known as *403(b)* plans. Contributions to both traditional 401(k) and 403(b) plans are deductible on both your federal and state taxes in the year that you make them. Employees of nonprofit organizations can generally contribute up to 20 percent or $23,500 of their salaries, whichever is less.

  TIP

  There's a benefit in addition to the up-front and ongoing tax benefits of these retirement savings plans: Some employers match your contributions. (If you're an employee in a small business, you can establish your own SEP-IRA.) Of course, the challenge for many people is to reduce their spending enough to be able to sock away these kinds of contributions.

  Some employers are offering a Roth 401(k) account, which, like a Roth IRA (discussed next), offers employees the ability to contribute on an after-tax basis. Withdrawals from such accounts generally aren't taxed in retirement.

  If you're self-employed, you can establish your own retirement savings plans for yourself and any employees you have. *Simplified Employee Pension-Individual Retirement Accounts* (SEP-IRA) allow you to put away up to 20 percent of your self-employment income up to an annual maximum of $70,000 (for tax year 2025).

  **Individual Retirement Accounts:** If you work for a company that doesn't offer a retirement savings plan, or if you've exhausted contributions to your company's plan, consider an *Individual Retirement Account* (IRA). Anyone who earns employment income or receives alimony may contribute up to $7,000 annually to an IRA (or the amount of your employment income or alimony income, if it's less than $7,000 in a year). A nonworking spouse may contribute up to $7,000 annually to a spousal IRA.

Your contributions to an IRA may or may not be tax-deductible. For tax year 2025, if you're single and your adjusted gross income is $77,000 or less for the year, you can deduct your full IRA contribution. If you're married and you file your taxes jointly, you're entitled to a full IRA deduction if your AGI is $123,000 per year or less.

TIP

If you can't deduct your contribution to a standard IRA account, consider making a contribution to a nondeductible IRA account called a *Roth IRA.* Single taxpayers with an AGI less than $150,000 and joint filers with an AGI less than $236,000 can contribute up to $7,000 per year to a Roth IRA. Although the contribution isn't deductible, earnings inside the account are shielded from taxes, and unlike withdrawals from a standard IRA, qualified withdrawals from a Roth IRA account are free from income tax.

TIP

Should you be earning a high enough income that you can't fund a Roth IRA, there's an indirect "backdoor" way to fund a Roth IRA. First, you contribute to a regular IRA as a nondeductible contribution. Then, you can convert your regular IRA contribution into a Roth IRA. Please note that this so-called backdoor method generally only makes sense if you don't have other money already invested in a regular IRA, because in that case, you can't simply withdraw your most recent contribution and not owe any tax.

You may invest the money in your IRA or self-employed plan retirement account (SEP-IRAs and so on) in stocks, bonds, mutual funds, and some other common investments, including bank accounts. Mutual funds (offered in most employer-based plans) and exchange-traded funds (ETFs) are ideal choices because they offer diversification and professional management. See Chapter 5 for more on mutual funds and ETFs.

- **Annuities: Maxing out your retirement savings:** What if you have so much cash sitting around that after maxing out your contributions to retirement accounts, including your IRA, you still want to sock more away into a tax-advantaged account? Enter the annuity. *Annuities* are contracts that insurance companies back. If you, the investor (annuity holder), should die during the so-called accumulation phase (that is, before receiving payments from the annuity), your designated beneficiary is guaranteed reimbursement of the amount of your original investment.

Annuities, like IRAs, allow your capital to grow and compound tax-deferred. You defer taxes until you withdraw the money. Unlike an IRA, which has an annual contribution limit of a few thousand dollars, an annuity allows you to deposit as much as you want in any year — even millions of dollars, if you've got millions! As with a Roth IRA, however, you get no up-front tax deduction for your contributions.

WARNING

Because annuity contributions aren't tax-deductible, and because annuities carry higher annual operating fees to pay for the small amount of insurance that comes with them, don't consider contributing to one until you've fully exhausted your other retirement account investing options. Because of their higher annual expenses, annuities generally make sense only if you won't need the money for 15 or more years.

## Accessing retirement account money early

Once you place such money inside a retirement account, you can't generally access it before age 59½ without paying current income taxes and a penalty — 10 percent of the withdrawn amount in federal tax, plus whatever your state charges.

This poses some potential problems. First, money placed inside retirement accounts is typically not available for other uses, such as buying a car or starting a small business. Second, if an emergency arises and you need to tap the money, you'll get hit with paying current income taxes and penalties on amounts withdrawn.

TIP

You can use the following ways to avoid the early-withdrawal penalties that the tax authorities normally apply:

- You can make penalty-free withdrawals of up to $10,000 from IRAs for a first-time home purchase or higher educational expenses for you, your spouse, or your children (and even grandchildren).
- Some company retirement plans allow you to borrow against your balance. You're essentially loaning money to yourself, with the interest payments going back into your account.
- If you have major medical expenses (exceeding 10 percent of your income) or a disability, you may be exempt from the

penalties under certain conditions. (You will still owe ordinary income tax on withdrawals.)

- You may withdraw money before age 59½ if you do so in equal, annual installments based on your life expectancy. You generally must make such distributions for at least five years or until age 59½, whichever is later.

REMEMBER

If you lose your job and withdraw retirement account money simply because you need it to live on, the penalties do apply. If you're not working, however, and you're earning so little income that you need to access your retirement account, you would likely be in a relatively low tax bracket (see Chapter 9). The lower income taxes you pay (compared with the taxes you would have paid on that money had you not sheltered it in a retirement account in the first place) should make up for most, if not all, of the penalty.

## Taking advantage of retirement accounts

To take advantage of retirement savings plans and the tax savings that accompany them, you must spend less than you earn. Only then can you afford to contribute to these retirement savings plans, unless you already happen to have a stash of cash from previous savings or an inheritance.

WARNING

The common mistake that many younger adults make is neglecting to take advantage of retirement accounts because of their enthusiasm for spending or investing in nonretirement accounts. Not investing in tax-sheltered retirement accounts can cost you hundreds, perhaps thousands, of dollars per year in lost tax savings. Add that loss up over the many years that you work and save, and not taking advantage of these tax reduction accounts can easily cost you tens of thousands to hundreds of thousands of dollars in the long term.

The sooner you start to save, the less painful it is each year to save enough to reach your goals, because your contributions have more years to compound. Each decade you delay saving approximately doubles the percentage of your earnings that you need to save to meet your goals. If saving 5 percent per year in your early 20s gets you to your retirement goal, waiting until your 30s to start may mean socking away approximately 10 percent to reach that same goal; waiting until your 40s means saving 20 percent. Start saving and investing now!

IN THIS CHAPTER

» **Insuring your home, your car, and your property**

» **Evaluating your need for life insurance**

» **Seeing why most working people need disability coverage**

» **Discovering long-term care and your options for financing it**

» **Ensuring that your estate is handled as you want**

# Chapter 8
# Protecting Your Assets with Insurance

An important part of financial literacy means understanding the need to protect yourself from financial losses. Assets such as your home and auto are valuable, and the cost to replace them with money out of your own pocket could be financially catastrophic. Similarly, a lawsuit should someone be injured or killed in your home or because of your car could be financially devastating.

This chapter covers why, how, and for how much to insure your home, personal property, and vehicle. I also discuss excess liability insurance. Then I dive into the essentials regarding life and disability insurance you may need to protect your income. Last, I discuss long-term care insurance, and how to determine where your money will go in the event of your death.

# Protecting Your Castle (and Your Pokémon Collection)

If your home burns to the ground, a comprehensive homeowner's insurance policy should pay for the cost of rebuilding the home. Similarly, you need to protect your auto and shield yourself from excess liabilities. In this section, I describe the essential insurance coverage you need to protect these important assets.

## Insuring your home

In this section I explain what you need on a home insurance policy and what you don't and how to get the best value for your money. I walk you through the elements of a homeowner's insurance policy — get out yours if you own a home.

TIP

If you're renting, you may want to obtain a renter's policy for two major reasons. The first is to protect your personal property, and the second is for some liability protection.

Here are the major elements on a homeowner's policy:

- **Dwelling:** Your home insurer should determine approximately how much it would cost (based on size and cost per square foot) to rebuild your home should it be a total loss. Make sure that your policy comes with "guaranteed replacement cost" coverage. This makes the insurer pay for the full cost to rebuild your home should it cost more than the dwelling coverage portion of your policy. Please note, though, that different insurers define their guarantees differently. Most place some sort of a cap on the coverage — for example, at 20 or 30 percent above the dwelling coverage on your policy.
- **Other structures:** This covers separate structures such as a shed, fencing, or a freestanding garage. If this coverage is higher than necessary given the actual covered other structures on your land, ask the insurer about options to reduce this coverage amount.
- **Personal property:** This portion of the policy covers the contents of your home: furniture, clothing, personal possessions, and so on. The coverage amount is typically

derived as a portion (for example, three-quarters) of the dwelling portion of your policy. A good policy will cover the full cost to replace damaged items — be sure that this is what you're paying for or inquire about the cost of a rider to provide this benefit. Some insurers will allow you to reduce your coverage amount from their standard level if you feel that would adequately insure your personal property.

- **Loss of use:** This again is standard coverage and often a portion (for example, 20 percent) of the dwelling coverage. If you can't reasonably live in your home after it is damaged, this part of your policy will pay for you to rent and enjoy a similar standard of living.
- **Personal liability:** If someone sues you for an accident relating to your home, this portion of the policy kicks in. As with your auto insurance, you should have enough liability to protect at least twice your assets. For coverage greater than $500,000, you would typically get excess liability coverage in a separate policy (see the "Protecting against mega-liability: Umbrella insurance").
- **Medical payments to others:** This is standard on most policies and provides limited coverage for out-of-pocket costs for accidents on your property.

Sometimes the location you want or need to live in comes with the added risk of certain disasters happening. Be sure to get catastrophic coverage as needed in your area. When considering a given home, be sure to investigate the risk of flooding, hurricanes, earthquakes, and landslides.

TIP

If possible, buy a home at low risk for natural disasters. An excellent warning sign for high-risk property is if you have difficulty finding insurance and find only overly expensive coverage from one or two companies.

Prospective real estate buyers can also research environmental hazards and issues of a specific property they may buy. Environmental Data Resources produces an EDR Neighborhood Environmental Report, which costs $100. You can order a report through an "EDR certified" home inspector, but you need not order a home inspection from that inspector. Call 800-352-0050 or visit EDR's website at www.edrnet.com.

## Insuring your car

If your car is involved in an accident, auto insurance helps pay for the damage to the cars and property involved. It can also help pay for associated medical expenses. This section talks about what you should have and probably don't need on your auto insurance policies.

Locate a copy of your most recent auto insurance statement. Often called a *declaration*, this statement should detail your coverage types and amounts, and premiums (cost).

The following list goes through each of the elements of your policy:

- **Liability:** Auto accidents can harm other people and damage property, and for accidents in which you're at fault, you can be sued. The liability portion of your policy provides coverage for these claims and comes in varying amounts; for example, $15,000, $30,000, $50,000, $100,000, $300,000, and so on. This coverage amount is per accident. You should have liability coverage of at least two times the value of your assets. If you have significant assets, you can more cost-effectively pick up additional liability protection after $300,000 or $500,000 of liability coverage on your auto policy through an umbrella or excess liability policy (see the "Protecting against mega-liability: Umbrella insurance").
- **Medical payments:** This optional rider generally provides $5,000 or $10,000 in medical benefits to you or other passengers in your car for medical expenses not covered by their health insurance policy. This coverage is considered nonessential because it is capped at a relatively small amount, and if someone lacks health insurance, $5,000 or $10,000 in benefits won't cover much. If you're at fault and you're sued, your liability coverage will protect you and help pay for the medical expenses of the other party if you're deemed at fault.
- **Uninsured motorist:** This coverage allows you (and your vehicle's passengers) to be compensated for pain and suffering, lost wages, and out-of-pocket medical expenses when you're in an accident with an uninsured or underinsured motorist. Think of this coverage as buying liability coverage for the other party if they don't have sufficient

coverage. Once you have adequate health and disability insurance that would take care of lost wages and medical expenses in an accident, being able to collect for pain and suffering isn't really necessary.

- **Collision:** This provides reimbursement for damage done to your car in an accident. As with other types of insurance that you purchase, take the highest deductible (such as $500 or $1,000) you can comfortably live with. The deductible represents the amount of money that you must pay out of your own pocket if you have a loss for which you file a claim. A high deductible helps keep down the cost of your coverage and eliminates the hassle of filing small claims.
- **Other than collision:** Sometimes known as comprehensive coverage, this provides insurance for damage done to your car for things other than accidents. For example, if you're driving down the road and a rock skips off the road and cracks your windshield, or your car that is parked on the street is damaged by someone driving by or parking near you, this coverage will pay for damage after your deductible. As with collision coverage, to reduce your premiums, choose as high a deductible (such as $500 or $1,000) as you are comfortable with.
- **Other riders:** Other typical add-ons that insurers and agents may put on your policy include towing, rental car reimbursement, and so on. Skip these because they ultimately cover small potential dollar items and aren't worth insuring for. Spend your insurance money on protecting against the big potential losses.

## Protecting against mega-liability: Umbrella insurance

*Umbrella insurance* (which is also referred to as *excess liability insurance*) is liability insurance that's added on top of the liability protection on your home and car(s). If, for example, you have $700,000 in assets, you can buy a $1 million umbrella liability policy to add to the $300,000 liability insurance that you have on your home and car. Expect to pay a couple hundred dollars — a small cost for big protection. Each year, thousands of people suffer lawsuits of more than $1 million related to their cars and homes.

Umbrella insurance is generally sold in increments of $1 million. So how do you decide how much you need if you have a lot of assets? You should have at least enough liability insurance to protect your assets and preferably enough to cover twice the value of those assets. To purchase umbrella insurance, start by contacting your existing homeowner's or auto insurance company.

## Assessing Your Need for Life Insurance

The primary reason to consider buying life insurance is to provide financially for those who are dependent on your employment income. However, just because you have a job, earn employment income, and have dependents (children, a spouse, and so on) doesn't mean that you need life insurance.

I'm not a fan of general rules like getting ten times your annual income in life insurance coverage, especially for those approaching or already in their senior years. Each person's circumstances can vary tremendously among many factors, such as

- **Your assets:** Generally speaking, the more you have relative to your income, spending, and obligations, the less life insurance you need.
- **Your debts:** Of course, not all debts are created equal. Debts on real estate or small businesses tend to have lower interest rates, and the interest is often tax-deductible. On the other hand, consumer debt — such as credit card and auto loan debt — tends to be at higher interest rates, and the interest generally isn't tax-deductible. Overall, the more total debt you have, the more life insurance you're likely to need.
- **Your health and the health of your family members:** If you have major medical problems or have a family member who's ill or who has special needs, you may need more coverage.
- **The number of children you desire to put through college:** A four-year college education, especially at private schools, is a major expense. So, if you have kids to put through school — and they may attend costly schools — you could be talking some really big bucks. And you face even bigger bucks if you want to help them through graduate or professional school after college.

» **Whether you'll have elderly parents to assist:** Of course, this factor is difficult to predict, but you should have some sense of your parents' physical and financial health. If you don't, try to broach the topic in a sensitive fashion with them.

REMEMBER

If you're still working, aren't yet financially independent, and need your current and future employment income to keep up your current lifestyle — and you're saving toward your financial goals — life insurance probably is a good choice. If you have others depending on your continued employment income, you generally should get term life insurance coverage (which I discuss in the later section "Figuring out what type to buy").

## Determining how much life insurance you need

After completing your retirement planning (see Chapter 7), you should have the current financial information you need to begin your calculations for how much life insurance you need. Here's a quick and simple way to determine how much life insurance to consider buying:

1. **Determine your annual after-tax income (from working, not investments).**

   You can find this number on your tax return or W-2 form from the past year. (The reason you work with after-tax income is because life insurance death benefit payouts aren't taxed.)

2. **Determine the amount of money you need in order to replace your income for the appropriate number of years.**

   You can find this amount by simply using the information in Table 8-1.

3. **Consider your overall financial situation and whether you need to replace all your income over the time period you chose in Step 2.**

   High income earners who live well beneath their means may not want or need to replace all their income. If you're in this category and determine that you don't need to replace all your income, apply an appropriate percentage.

**TABLE 8-1 Calculating Your Life Insurance Needs**

| To Replace Your Income for This Many Years | Multiply Your Annual After-Tax Income by |
|---|---|
| 5 years | 5 |
| 10 years | 9 |
| 15 years | 12 |
| 20 years | 15 |
| 25 years | 17 |
| 30 years | 19 |

## Reviewing your current life coverage

Before you rush out to buy life insurance, make sure you first assess how much coverage you may have through your employer and through Social Security. The amount of coverage you have could reduce the amount you need to purchase independently. Employer-based life insurance coverage is an easier issue to deal with compared to Social Security survivor's benefits, so I address it first.

### Employer-based life insurance

Some employers offer life insurance coverage. If it's free, by all means factor it into your calculations for how much additional coverage you may need. (See the earlier section, "Determining how much life insurance you need," for more on calculating the coverage you need.)

For example, if your employer gives you $50,000 in life insurance without cost — and in Table 8-1 you calculated you should have $300,000 of coverage — simply subtract the $50,000 your employer provides to come up with $250,000 of life insurance you need to get on your own.

Keep in mind, however, that if you leave the employer, you'll most likely lose the provided insurance coverage. At that time, if your needs haven't changed, you'll need to replace the employer coverage.

TIP

If you have to pay out of your own pocket for employer-based life insurance, you can probably pay less elsewhere. That's because group life plans tend to cost more than the least expensive individual life insurance plans. Also, an individual policy that you buy isn't dependent upon staying with your current employer, so that's an additional reason to get your own coverage and not buy any through your current employer.

REMEMBER

Here's one important caveat: You must be in good health to get life insurance on your own (at a competitive price, if at all). If you have health problems, group coverage is likely to be your best bet.

## Social Security survivor's benefits

Social Security can provide survivor's benefits to your spouse and children. However, if your surviving spouse is working and earning an income comparable to yours, they're going to receive few to no survivor's benefits. Also keep in mind that Social Security survivor's benefits aren't paid to a surviving spouse until they're at least age 60.

Prior to reaching Social Security's full retirement age, or FRA, your survivor's benefits get reduced by $1 for every $2 you earn above $18,960 (the limit for 2021). This income threshold is higher if you reach FRA during the year. For example, the Social Security benefits of those reaching FRA during 2021 are reduced by $1 for each $3 they earn above $50,520 until the month in which they reach FRA.

If you or your spouse anticipate earning a low enough income to qualify for Social Security survivor's benefits, you may want to factor them into the amount of life insurance you calculate in Table 8-1. For example, suppose your annual after-tax income is $40,000 and Social Security provides a survivor's benefit of $15,000 annually. You calculate the annual amount of life insurance needed to replace like this: $40,000 – $15,000 = $25,000.

TIP

You also can set up a "my Social Security" account on the Social Security website (`www.ssa.gov`) that lets you obtain updated benefits estimates, verify your earnings, and take other actions. Or, you can contact the Social Security Administration (SSA) for the "Request For Social Security Statement," Form SSA-7004, which gives you an estimate of your Social Security benefits. You can request this form on their website or by calling the SSA at 800-772-1213.

## Figuring out what type to buy

When looking to buy life insurance, you basically have two choices: term life insurance and cash value insurance. The following sections outline these two options and their differences and help you determine which may be better for your circumstance.

### Term life insurance

*Term life insurance* is pure life insurance protection. It's 100 percent life insurance protection with nothing else, and, frankly, in my opinion, it's the way to go for the vast majority of people. Agents typically sell term life insurance as so-called "temporary" coverage, which is just fine because life insurance is not a permanent need during certain years of life when others are financially dependent on your employment earnings.

Remember that the cost of life insurance increases as you get older. You can purchase term life insurance so that your premium steps up annually or after 5, 10, 15, or 20 years. The less frequently your premium adjusts, the higher the initial premium and its incremental increases will be.

The advantage of a premium that locks in for more years is that you have the security of knowing how much you'll be paying over that time period. You also don't need to go through medical evaluations as frequently to qualify for the lowest rate possible. Policies that adjust the premium every five to ten years offer a happy medium between price and predictability.

WARNING

The disadvantage of a term life insurance policy with a long-term rate lock is that you pay more in the early years than you do on a policy that adjusts more frequently. Also, your life insurance needs are likely to change over time. So, you may throw money away when you dump a policy with a long-term premium guarantee before its rate is set to change.

REMEMBER

Be sure that you get a policy that's guaranteed renewable. This feature assures that the policy can't be canceled because of poor health. Unless you expect that your life insurance needs will disappear when the policy is up for renewal, be sure to buy a life insurance policy with the guaranteed renewable feature.

### Cash value coverage

*Cash value* coverage, also referred to as *whole life insurance*, combines life insurance protection with an investment account. For a given level of coverage, cash value coverage costs substantially more than term coverage, and some of this extra money goes into a low-interest investment account for you. This coverage appeals to people who don't like to feel that they're wasting money on an insurance policy they hope to never use.

Agents usually sell cash value life insurance as permanent protection. The reality is that people who buy term insurance generally hold it as long as they have people financially dependent on them (which usually isn't a permanent situation). People who buy cash value insurance are more likely to hold onto their coverage until they die.

WARNING

Insurance agents often pitch cash value life insurance over term life insurance. Cash value life insurance costs much more and provides fatter profits for insurance companies and commissions to the agents who sell it. So, don't be swayed to purchase this type unless you really need it.

Cash value life insurance can serve a purpose if you have a substantial net worth that would cause you to be subject to estate taxes. Under current tax law (which could, of course, change), you can leave up to $13.99 million — free of federal estate taxes — to your heirs. Buying a cash value policy and placing it in an irrevocable life insurance trust allows the policy's death benefits to pass to your heirs free of federal estate taxes.

## Choosing where to buy life insurance

If you're going to purchase life insurance, you need to know where to go. You can look at the following two places:

- **Local insurance agents:** Many local insurance agents sell life insurance, and you certainly can obtain quotes and a policy through them. As with any major purchase, it's a good idea to shop around. Don't get quotes from just one agent. Contact at least three. It costs you nothing to ask for a quote, and you'll probably be surprised at the differences in premiums.

REMEMBER

As I discuss earlier in this chapter, many agents prefer to sell cash value policies because of the fatter commissions on those policies. So, don't be persuaded to purchase that type of policy if you don't really think it's right for you.

- **An insurance agency quote service:** The best of these services provides proposals from the highest-rated, lowest-cost companies available. Like other agencies, the service receives a commission if you buy a policy from them, but you're under no obligation to do so.

  To get a quote, these services ask you your date of birth, whether you smoke, some basic health questions, and how much coverage you want. Services that are worth considering include the following:

  - **AccuQuote:** www.accuquote.com; 800-442-9899
  - **ReliaQuote:** www.reliaquote.com; 800-940-3002
  - **Term4Sale:** www.term4sale.com; 888-798-3488
  - **USAA:** www.usaa.com; 800-531-8722 (this company sells low-cost term life insurance directly to the public; some of its other insurance products are only available to members of the military and their families)

# Protecting Your Employment Income: Disability Insurance

*Long-term disability* (LTD) insurance replaces a portion of your lost income in the event that a disability prevents you from working either permanently or temporarily for an extended period of time. For example, you may be in an accident or develop a medical condition that keeps you from working for six months or longer. During your working years, your future income earning ability is likely your most valuable asset — far more valuable than a car or even your home. Your ability to produce income should be protected or insured.

REMEMBER

Even if you don't have dependents, you probably still need disability coverage. After all, aren't *you* dependent on your income?

If you want to protect your future employment income, an LTD plan is one of the best ways to do so. Here are some reasons you should have LTD:

- **Life is uncertain.** You can't know when and what type of disability you may suffer. That's because many disabilities are caused by medical problems (arthritis, cerebral palsy, diabetes, glaucoma, multiple sclerosis, muscular dystrophy, stroke, and so on) and accidents (head injuries, spinal injury, loss of limb, and so on). Although older folks are at greater risk for more severe medical problems, plenty of younger adults suffer accidents or major medical problems leading to disability.
- **Many applicants for Social Security disability benefits coverage are turned down.** You can receive payments only if your disability will result in death or if you aren't able to perform any substantial, gainful activity for more than a year. Recent studies show that only about 35 percent of applicants for Social Security disability benefits are approved.
- **Even if you do qualify, your state's disability plan and Social Security insurance programs probably won't provide you with sufficient coverage, especially if you're a higher income earner.** State programs typically only pay benefits for one year or less, which isn't going to cut it if you truly suffer a long-term disability that lasts for years. While one year of coverage is better than none, the premiums for such short-term coverage often are higher per dollar of benefit than through the best private insurer programs.

  Similarly, although Social Security disability benefits can be paid long term, remember that these payments are only intended to provide for basic subsistence living expenses. Those earning more than $50,000 per year find that less than half of their income is replaced by Social Security disability payments. The higher your income, the smaller the portion of your income will be replaced by Social Security disability.
- **Worker's compensation, if you have coverage through your employer, won't pay benefits at all if you get injured or become sick away from your job.** Such narrow coverage that only pays benefits under a limited set of circumstances isn't the comprehensive disability insurance you need.

## Identifying needed disability coverage

Unless you're already financially independent, you need long-term disability insurance during your working years. Generally speaking, you should have LTD coverage that provides a benefit of approximately 60 percent of your gross income. Because disability benefits payments are tax-free if you pay the premium for disability insurance you buy, they should replace your current after-tax earnings. If you earn a high income and spend far less than that, you may be fine purchasing a monthly benefit amount that's less than 60 percent of your income.

REMEMBER

I recommend that your disability policy contain the following:

- **An "own occupation" definition of disability:** This definition allows you to collect benefits if you can't perform your regular occupation. For example, if you work as an accountant, your disability policy shouldn't require you to take a job as a retail worker if you no longer can perform the duties of an accountant.
- **A noncancelable and guaranteed renewable clause:** This clause guarantees that your policy can't be canceled if you develop health problems. If you purchase a policy that requires periodic physical exams, you could lose your coverage when you're most likely to need it.
- **A financially appropriate benefit period:** Obtain a policy that pays benefits until an age at which you would become financially self-sufficient. For most people, that would require obtaining a policy that pays benefits to age 65 or 67 (when full Social Security retirement benefits begin).

  If you're close to being financially independent and expect to accomplish that or retire before your mid-60s, consider a policy that pays benefits for five years.
- **A high deductible/waiting period:** The *waiting period* is the "deductible" on disability insurance. It's the time between your disability and when you can begin collecting benefits. I recommend that you take the longest waiting period that your financial circumstances allow, because doing so will greatly reduce your policy's premiums. I generally recommend a waiting period of at least 90 or 180 days.

» **Residual benefits:** This feature pays you a partial benefit if you have a disability that prevents you from working full time.

» **Cost-of-living adjustments:** This provision automatically increases your benefit payment after you're disabled by a set percentage or in step with inflation.

## Shopping for disability coverage

After you understand the importance of having good disability insurance, I hope that you'll be motivated to close the deal and buy it. Here are some ways to shop and compare so that you end up with good coverage at a competitive price:

» **Check with your employer.** Group disability plans can greatly accelerate your shopping process and generally offer decent value. Unlike with life insurance plans, group disability plans tend to offer more bang for your buck.

» **Peruse professional associations.** For many self-employed people, if you find the associations that exist for your occupation or profession, you may well discover a fine disability plan. Just be sure to compare their offerings to whatever individual policy proposals you find.

» **Avail yourself of agents.** Get referrals to insurance agents in your area who specialize in disability insurance. Using the policy guidelines in the preceding section, "Identifying needed disability coverage," solicit and evaluate proposals.

REMEMBER

The insurance company you choose should have strong financial health with the leading credit rating agencies.

# Understanding Long-Term Care

*Long-term care* may mean something different to every person. Basically, the term covers any assistance you may need with your day-to-day living. The forms of long-term care depend on the level of assistance you need.

## Naming the types of long-term care

Following are the five levels of care, from least to most care:

- **Independent living:** These facilities don't offer LTC, but they're considered by those who no longer want to live completely on their own. The facilities generally are apartments for those seniors who can live on their own and whose only need is light housekeeping. Independent living facilities often offer a number of group activities, activity rooms, recreation facilities, and transportation to local shopping malls, doctors' offices, and other locations. With independent living, you don't receive any medical care and only receive minimal services, though other services often are available for additional fees.
- **Home care:** Most people want to stay in their homes for as long as possible. In home care, an agency often assigns its employees to people needing care. Many people, however, receive home care from family and friends who provide unskilled assistance, often without compensation. Home care may be provided for anywhere from a few hours weekly to 24 hours a day, seven days a week. Home care can consist of personal services, such as cooking and cleaning, provided by a home health aide. It also can consist of skilled medical care, often provided by a nurse or other licensed professional.
- **Assisted living:** Assisted living often is confused with nursing home care. Many people think they're interchangeable, but they aren't. Assisted living usually is delivered in an apartment-like building that has on-site services such as dining, physical therapy, and limited nursing care, along with a range of social and recreational activities. Assisted living is for those who need some help with one or more activities of daily living (ADL) but don't need skilled nursing care or a lot of help, attention, or rehabilitation.

  REMEMBER

  In most states, assisted living facilities usually are less regulated and aren't required to have significant nursing or other medical care on the premises.
- **Nursing homes:** A nursing home provides a wide variety of services ranging from feeding, dressing, and bathing residents to monitoring medical conditions and providing

significant medical care. They also provide physical therapy. In addition to support staff, a nursing home has a large number of healthcare workers, ranging from nurse's aides to registered nurses. Nursing homes usually are heavily regulated and are inspected annually by state regulators.

- **Memory care:** Memory care is a hybrid of assisted living and a nursing home. Memory care is intended for someone with an advanced level of reduced cognitive function, such as dementia or Alzheimer's disease. Memory care units can be found in assisted living facilities and nursing homes.

After considering the type of care you need and want, you also can look at the different ways care is provided. The following are three frequent ways of providing the care:

- **Continuing care communities:** These multipurpose communities offer several different kinds of senior care facilities in one location, usually independent living, assisted living, and a nursing home. You pay a large fee when entering the community, plus monthly charges. As you age and more care is needed, you can shift from independent living to assisted living to a nursing home. Admission at each level of care is guaranteed when you need it.

  TIP

  A big advantage of continuing care facilities to married couples is that if one spouse needs to move to a higher level of care, the other is living a short walk away in the same community.

- **Group homes:** For those who don't want an institutional-like setting, a group home provides assisted living services (or less) in a single-family home or similar structure. In most states, these types of homes undergo a very low level of regulation when the number of residents stays below a maximum level, usually from 5 to 15.
- **Stand-alone facilities:** These tend to be large facilities that provide one or two types of care, such as a nursing home or an assisted living facility with an independent living or memory care section. When you need a different type of care, you have to move to a different facility. For example, you may start in an assisted living facility and after a period of years need a higher level of care. You then have to move to a nursing home.

## Predicting who will need long-term care

You may not need LTC, and if you do ultimately need it, LTC usually isn't a stereotypical multiyear stay in a nursing home. In fact, the odds of needing extended, extensive LTC in a nursing home are lower than most people think — but not negligible. Yet, care at home or in an assisted living facility is more likely and will last longer than most nursing home stays. In fact, the use of these services is growing.

REMEMBER

If you're among the minority who do need extended LTC, the cost could rapidly deplete your savings and your estate; the average outcomes will no longer matter. So to avoid depleting your savings and other assets, you need to plan for how to finance potential LTC costs.

## Planning to pay for LTC

The potential cost of LTC is a mystery to most Americans. They think that it's expensive, but they don't know how expensive. So when considering and planning for LTC, you want to have a good idea of how much it costs in case you (or your spouse) should need it. Fortunately, the quality of cost estimates has improved in recent years. Even so, you have to use surveys and estimates of the costs carefully.

Putting together a clear plan for how you're going to finance LTC is an important decision. You basically have five ways you can pay for any LTC you may need:

- **Medicare:** Medicare is the healthcare financing program for those age 65 and over. Its LTC coverage is limited to short-term stays needed for rehabilitation and for some services provided in an LTC facility.
- **Medicaid:** Medicaid is a program for the poor and will provide nursing home coverage only for seniors with limited income and assets. It doesn't cover assisted living.
- **Private traditional insurance:** A traditional LTCI policy can be an individual policy or a group policy, which usually is purchased through your employer.
- **Hybrid policies:** Many annuities and cash value life insurance policies offer LTC riders. The annuity balance or life insurance cash value account is used to pay for LTC when needed, and

the insurer pays for more care up to a limit, if that's needed. If LTC isn't needed, your loved ones eventually receive the annuity balance or life insurance benefit. These often are referred to as hybrid, linked-benefit, or asset-linked policies.

- **Personal funds:** These are your (and your family's) savings and investments. Using this source to pay for LTC often is called *self-financing.* Any LTC not paid for by the other sources will be paid from personal funds. I review investments in Chapter 5.

# Estate Planning: Passing the Torch to Future You

*Estate planning* is the process of determining what will happen to your assets after you die. Considering your mortality in the context of insurance may seem a bit odd. But the time and cost of various estate-planning maneuvers is really nothing more than buying insurance: You're ensuring that, after you die, everything will be taken care of as you wish, and taxes will be minimized. Thinking about estate planning in this way can help you better evaluate whether certain options make sense at particular points in your life.

Depending upon your circumstances, you may eventually want to contact an attorney who specializes in estate-planning matters. However, educating yourself first about the different options is worth your time. More than a few attorneys have their own agendas about what you should do, so be careful. And most of the estate-planning strategies that you're likely to benefit from don't require hiring an attorney.

## Wills, living wills, and medical powers of attorney

When you have children who are minors (dependents), a will is a necessity. The will names the guardian to whom you entrust your children if both you and your spouse die. Should you and your spouse both die without a will (called *intestate*), the state (courts and social-service agencies) decides who will raise your children. Therefore, even if you can't decide at this time who you want to raise your children, you should *at least* appoint a trusted guardian who can decide for you.

Having a will makes good sense even if you don't have kids, because it gives instructions on how to handle and distribute all your worldly possessions. If you die without a will, your state decides how to distribute your money and other property, according to state law. Therefore, your friends, distant relatives, and favorite charities will probably receive nothing. Without any living relatives, your money may go to the state government!

Without a will, your heirs are legally powerless, and the state may appoint an administrator to supervise the distribution of your assets at a fee of around 5 percent of your estate. A bond typically must also be posted at a cost of several hundred dollars.

A living will and a medical power of attorney are useful additions to a standard will. A *living will* (also known as an advanced healthcare directive) tells your doctor what, if any, life-support measures you prefer. A *medical* (or *healthcare*) *power of attorney* grants authority to someone you trust to make decisions regarding your medical care options.

The simplest and least costly way to prepare a will, a living will, and a medical power of attorney is to use a high-quality, user-friendly software package, such as Quicken WillMaker & Trust by Nolo. Be sure to give copies of these documents to the guardians and executors named in the documents. You don't need an attorney to make a legal will. Most attorneys, in fact, prepare wills and living trusts using software packages! What makes a will valid is that three people witness your signing of it.

TIP

If preparing the will all by yourself seems overwhelming, you can (instead of hiring an attorney) use a paralegal typing service to help you prepare the documents. These services generally charge 50 percent or less of what an attorney charges.

## Avoiding probate through living trusts

Because of the United States' quirky legal system, even if you have a will, some or all of your assets must go through a court process known as probate. *Probate* is the legal process for administering and implementing the directions in a will. Property and assets that are owned in joint tenancy or inside retirement accounts, such as IRAs or 401(k)s, generally pass to heirs without having to go through probate. However, most other assets are probated.

A *living trust* effectively transfers assets into a trust. As the trustee, you control those assets, and you can revoke the trust whenever you desire. The advantage of a living trust is that upon your death, assets can pass directly to your beneficiaries without going through probate. Probate can be a lengthy, expensive hassle for your heirs — with legal fees tallying 5 percent or more of the value of the estate. In addition, your assets become a matter of public record as a result of probate.

Living trusts are likely to be of greatest value to people who meet one or more of the following criteria (the more that apply, the more value trusts have):

- Age 60 or older
- Single
- Assets worth more than $100,000 that must pass through probate (including real estate, nonretirement accounts, and small businesses)
- Real property held in other states

As with a will, you do *not* need an attorney to establish a legal and valid living trust. (You can use software such as Quicken WillMaker & Trust by Nolo or consider the paralegal services that I mention in the preceding section.) Attorney fees for establishing a living trust can range from hundreds to thousands of dollars. Hiring an attorney is of greatest value to people with large estates (see the next section) who don't have the time, desire, and expertise to maximize the value derived from estate planning. Also consult with an attorney if you have nonstandard wishes to be carried out, such as special-needs beneficiaries or extra control measures you want applied to assets after incapacity or death.

*Note:* Living trusts keep assets out of probate but have nothing to do with minimizing estate or inheritance taxes.

## Reducing estate taxes

Under current tax laws, an individual can pass $13.99 million to beneficiaries without having to pay federal estate taxes (married couples can pass $27.98 million).

Whether you should be concerned about possible estate taxes depends on several issues. How much of your assets you're going to use up during your life is the first and most important issue you need to consider. This amount depends on how much your assets grow over time, as well as how rapidly you spend money. During retirement, you'll (hopefully) be using at least some of your money.

I've seen too many affluent individuals, especially in their retirements, worry about estate taxes on their assets. If your intention is to leave your money to your children, grandchildren, or a charity, why not start giving while you're still alive so that you can enjoy the act? You can give $19,000 annually to each of your beneficiaries, *tax-free*. By giving away money, you reduce your estate and, therefore, the estate taxes owed on it. Any appreciation on the value of the gift between the date of the gift and your date of death is also out of your estate and not subject to estate taxes.

In addition to gifting, a number of trusts allow you to minimize estate taxes. Although it's no longer generally necessary at the federal level, you may want to establish a *bypass trust* to effectively double the estate tax limit for your state. Upon the death of the first spouse, assets held in their name go into the bypass trust, effectively removing those assets from the remaining spouse's taxable estate. (Speak with an estate-planning attorney.)

Cash value life insurance is another estate-planning tool. Unfortunately, it's a tool that's overused or, I should say, oversold. People who sell cash value insurance — that is, insurance salespeople and others masquerading as financial planners — too often advocate life insurance as the one and only way to reduce estate taxes. Other methods for reducing estate taxes are usually superior, because they don't require wasting money on life insurance.

Small-business owners whose businesses are worth several million dollars or more may want to consider cash value life insurance under specialized circumstances. If you lack the necessary additional assets to pay expected estate taxes and you don't want your beneficiaries to be forced to sell the business, you can buy cash value life insurance to pay expected estate taxes. To find out more about how to reduce your estate (and other) taxes, visit my website at `www.erictyson.com`.

IN THIS CHAPTER

» Viewing your finances holistically

» Steering clear of common mistakes

» Overcoming tax-planning hurdles

# Chapter 9
# Making Tax-Wise Personal Finance Decisions

Financial literacy requires much more than knowing how to invest money. It includes managing your personal finances such that all the pieces of your financial life fit together. And, just like designing a vacation itinerary, managing your personal finances means developing a strategy to make the best use of your limited dollars and being prepared to deal with some adversity and changes to the landscape. Getting a handle on the things you can plan for — like your taxes — is a big part of effective financial planning.

## Considering Taxes in Your Financial Planning

Taxes are a large and vital piece of your financial puzzle. The following list shows some of the ways that tax issues are involved in making sound financial decisions throughout the year:

- **Spending:** The more you spend, the more taxes you'll pay for taxed purchases and for being less able to take advantage of the many benefits in the tax code that require you to have money to invest in the first place. For example, contrary to the hucksters on late-night infomercials, you need money to purchase real estate, which offers many tax benefits. And because taxes are probably your largest or second biggest expenditure, a budget that overlooks tax-reduction strategies is likely doomed to fail. Unless you have wealthy, benevolent relatives, you may be stuck with a lifetime of working if you can't save money.
- **Retirement accounts:** Taking advantage of retirement accounts can mean tens, perhaps even hundreds, of thousands more dollars in your pocket come retirement time.
- **Investing:** Merely choosing investments that generate healthy rates of return isn't enough. What matters is not what you make but what you keep — after paying taxes. Understand and capitalize on the many tax breaks available to investors in stocks, bonds, mutual funds, exchange-traded funds, real estate, and your own business.
- **Protecting your assets:** Some of your insurance decisions also affect the taxes you pay. You'd think that after a lifetime of tax payments, your heirs would be left alone when you pass on to the great beyond — wishful thinking. Estate planning can significantly reduce the taxes to be siphoned off from your estate.

Taxes infiltrate many areas of your personal finances. Some people make important financial decisions without considering taxes (and other important variables). Conversely, in an obsession to minimize or avoid taxes, other people make decisions that are counterproductive to achieving their long-term personal and financial goals. Although this chapter shows you that taxes are an important component to factor into your major financial decisions, taxes should not drive or dictate the decisions you make.

Table 9-1 shows the federal income tax brackets and rates.

**TABLE 9-1 2025 Federal Income Tax Brackets and Rates**

| Tax Rate Returns | For Single Filers | For Married Individuals Filing Joint Returns |
|---|---|---|
| 10% | $0 to $11,925 | $0 to $23,850 |
| 12% | $11,925 to $48,475 | $23,850 to $96,950 |
| 22% | $48,475 to $103,350 | $96,950 to $206,700 |
| 24% | $103,350 to $197,300 | $206,700 to $394,600 |
| 32% | $197,300 to $250,525 | $394,600 to $501,050 |
| 35% | $250,525 to $626,350 | $501,050 to $751,600 |
| 37% | $626,350 or more | $751,600 or more |

# Avoiding Common Tax Mistakes

Even if some parts of the tax system are hopelessly and unreasonably complicated, there's no reason why you can't learn from the mistakes of others to save yourself some money. With this goal in mind, this section details common tax blunders that people make when it comes to managing their money.

## Seeking advice after a major decision

Too many people come across information and hire help after making a decision, even though seeking preventive help ahead of time generally is wiser and less costly. Before making any major financial decisions, educate yourself. This book can help answer many of your questions.

TIP

If you're going to hire a tax advisor to give advice, do so before making your decision(s). The wrong move when selling a piece of real estate or taking money from a retirement account can cost you thousands of dollars in taxes!

## Failing to withhold enough taxes

WARNING

If you're self-employed or earn significant taxable income from investments outside retirement accounts, you need to be making estimated quarterly tax payments. Likewise, if, during the year, you sell an investment at a profit, you may need to make a (higher) quarterly tax payment.

Not having a human resources department to withhold taxes from their pay as they earn it, some self-employed people dig themselves into a perpetual tax hole by failing to submit estimated quarterly tax payments. They get behind in their tax payments during their first year of self-employment and thereafter are always playing catch-up. People often don't discover that they "should've" paid more taxes during the year until after they complete their returns in the spring — or get penalty notices from the IRS and their states. Then they have to come up with sizable sums all at once. Don't be a "should've" victim.

TIP

Although I — and the IRS — want you to keep your taxes current during the year, I don't want you to overpay. Some people have too much tax withheld during the year, and this overpayment can go on year after year. Although it may feel good to get a sizable refund check every spring, why should you loan your money to the government interest-free? If you work for an employer, you can complete a new W-4 to adjust your withholding. Turn the completed W-4 in to your employer. If you're self-employed, complete Form 1040-ES. You can find current and past year's tax forms at `https://www.irs.gov`.

## Overlooking legitimate deductions

Some taxpayers miss out on perfectly legal tax deductions because they just don't know about them. Ignorance is not bliss when it comes to your income taxes . . . it's costly. If you aren't going to take the time to discover the legitimate deductions available to you, spring for the cost of a competent tax advisor at least once.

Fearing an audit, some taxpayers (and even some tax preparers) avoid taking deductions that they have every right to take. Unless you have something to hide, such behavior is foolish and costly. Remember that a certain number of returns are randomly audited every year, so even when you don't take every deduction to which you're legally entitled, you may nevertheless get audited!

TIP

How bad is an audit, really? An hour or so with the IRS is not as bad as you may think. It may be worth the risk of claiming all the tax breaks to which you're entitled, especially when you consider the amounts you can save through the years.

## Passing up retirement accounts

All the tax deductions and tax deferrals that come with accounts such as 401(k)s, 403(b)s, SEP-IRAs, and IRAs were put in the tax code to encourage you to save for retirement. So why not take advantage of the benefits?

You probably have your reasons or excuses, but most excuses for missing out on this strategy just don't make good financial sense. People often underfund retirement accounts because they spend too much and because retirement seems so far away. Many people also mistakenly believe that retirement account money is totally inaccessible until they're old enough to qualify for senior discounts.

## Ignoring tax considerations when investing

Suppose that you want to unload some stock so that you can buy a new car. You sell an investment at a significant profit and feel good about your financial genius. But, come tax time, you may feel differently.

REMEMBER

Don't forget to consider the taxes due on profits from the sale of investments (except those in retirement accounts) when making decisions about what to sell and when to sell it. Your tax situation should also factor in what you invest outside retirement accounts. When you're in a relatively high tax bracket, you probably don't want investments that pay much in taxable distributions such as taxable interest, which only add to your tax burden.

## Not buying a home

In the long run, owning a home should cost you less than renting. And because mortgage interest and property taxes may be partially deductible, the government, in effect, subsidizes the cost of home ownership.

Even if the government didn't help you with tax benefits when buying and owning a home, you'd still be better off owning over your adult life. If you rent instead, all your housing expenses are exposed to inflation, unless you have a great rent-controlled deal. So owning your own abode makes good financial and tax sense. And don't let the lack of money for a down payment stand in your way — methods exist for buying real estate with little up-front money.

## Allowing your political views to distort your decision making

To be a successful investor and make sound financial decisions, try to leave your political beliefs out of it and be unemotional. Extreme changes rarely occur even when one party rules for a couple of years in Washington, D.C. It's often soon replaced by divided government, which leads to more incremental change and eventually a switch in power back to the currently out-of-power party.

## Ignoring the financial aid (tax) system

WARNING

The college financial aid system in this country assumes that the money you save outside tax-sheltered retirement accounts is available to pay educational expenses. As a result, families who save money outside instead of inside retirement accounts may qualify for far less "financial aid" than they otherwise would. Financial aid is actually a misnomer because what colleges and universities are doing is charging a different price to different families after analyzing their finances. So, when a college appears to be giving you money, what they're actually doing is reducing their inflated prices to a more reasonable level.

If you're affluent and have done a good job saving and investing money, colleges are generally going to charge you more. So in addition to normal income taxes, an extra financial aid "tax" is effectively exacted. Be sure to read Chapter 7, which covers the best ways to save and invest for educational costs.

## Neglecting the timing of events you can control

The amount of tax you pay on certain transactions can vary, depending on the timing of events. If you're nearing retirement, for example, you may soon be in a lower tax bracket. To the extent possible, you should consider delaying and avoid claiming investment income until your overall income level drops, and you need to take as many deductions or losses as you can now while your income is still high. Following are two tax-reducing strategies — income shifting and bunching or shifting deductions — that you may be able to put to good use when you can control the timing of either your income or deductions.

## Shifting income

Suppose that your employer tells you in late December that you're eligible for a bonus. You find out that you have the option of receiving your bonus in either December or January (ask your payroll and benefits department if this is an option). Looking ahead, if you're pretty certain that you're going to be in a higher tax bracket next year, request to receive your bonus in December.

Or suppose that you run your own business and operate on a cash accounting basis and think that you'll be in a lower tax bracket next year. Perhaps business has slowed of late or you plan to take time off to be with a newborn or take an extended trip. You can send out some invoices later in the year so that your customers won't pay you until January, which falls in the next tax year.

## Bunching or shifting deductions

When the total of your itemized deductions on Schedule A is lower than the standard deduction, you need to take the standard deduction. This itemized deduction total is worth checking each year, because you may have more deductions in some years than others, and you may occasionally be able to itemize.

When you can control the timing of payment of particular expenses that are eligible for itemizing, you can shift or bunch more of them into select years when you're more likely to have enough deductions to take advantage of itemizing. Suppose that because you don't have many itemized deductions this year, you use the standard deduction. Late in the year, however, you feel certain that you'll itemize next year, because you plan to buy a home and will therefore be able to claim significant mortgage interest and some property tax deductions. It makes sense, then, to shift and bunch as many deductible expenses as possible into next year. For example, if you're getting ready to make a tax-deductible donation of old clothes and household goods to charity, wait until January to do so.

In any tax year that you're sure you won't have enough deductions to be able to itemize, shift as many itemizable expenses as you can into the next tax year. To find out which types of expenses you can itemize, see the latest edition of my book *Taxes For Dummies* (Wiley).

WARNING

Be careful when using your credit card to pay expenses. These expenses must be recognized for tax purposes in the year in which the charge was made on the card and not when you actually pay the credit card bill.

## Not using tax advisors effectively

If your financial situation is complicated, going it alone and relying only on the IRS instructions to figure your taxes usually is a mistake. Many people find the IRS publications tedious and not geared toward highlighting opportunities for tax reductions.

Instead, you can start by reading the relevant sections of this book. You can figure out taxes for yourself, or you can hire a tax advisor to figure them out for you. Doing nothing isn't an advisable option!

TIP

When you're overwhelmed by the complexity of particular financial decisions, get advice from tax and financial advisors who sell their time and nothing else. Protect yourself by checking references and clarifying what advice, analysis, and recommendations the advisor will provide for the fee charged. If your tax situation is complicated, you'll probably more than recoup a preparer's fee, as long as you take the time to hire a good advisor.

TIP

Remember that using a tax advisor is most beneficial when you face new tax questions or problems. If your tax situation remains complicated, or if you know that you'd do a worse job on your own, by all means keep using a tax preparer. But don't pay a big fee year after year to a tax advisor who simply plugs your numbers into the tax forms. If your situation is unchanging or isn't that complicated, consider hiring and paying someone to figure out your taxes one time. After that, go ahead and try completing your own tax return.

# Understanding Why People Make Bad Tax Decisions

When bad things happen, it's usually for a variety of reasons. And so it is with making financial blunders that cause you to pay more tax dollars. The following sections describe some common culprits that may be keeping you from making tax-wise financial maneuvers and what you can do about them.

## Getting bad advice

Wanting to hire a financial advisor to help you make better financial decisions is a logical inclination, especially if you're a time-starved person. But when you pick a poor planner or someone who isn't a financial planner but rather a salesperson in disguise, watch out!

WARNING

Unfortunately, many people calling themselves financial planners, financial consultants, or financial advisors actually work on commission, which creates enormous conflicts of interest with providing unbiased and objective financial advice. Brokers and commission-based financial planners (who are also therefore brokers) structure their advice around selling you investment and other financial products that provide them with commissions. As a result, they tend to take a narrow view of your finances and frequently ignore the tax and other consequences of financial moves. Or they may pitch the supposed tax benefits of an investment they're eager to sell you as a reason for you to buy it. It may provide a tax benefit for someone, but not necessarily for you in your specific situation.

The few planners who work on a fee basis primarily provide money-management services and typically charge about 1 percent per year of the money they manage. Fee-based planners have their own conflicts of interest, because all things being equal, they want you to hire them to manage your money. Therefore, they can't objectively help you decide whether you should pay off your mortgage and other debts, invest in real estate or a small business, or invest more in your employer's retirement plan. In short, they have a bias against financial strategies that take your investment money out of their hands.

WARNING

Be especially leery of planners, brokers, and money-managing planners who lobby you to sell investments that you've held for a while and that show a profit. If you sell these investments, you may have a hefty tax burden. (See Chapter 5 for more insight on how to make these important investing decisions.)

## Misleading advertising

Another reason you may make tax missteps in managing your personal finances is advertising. Although reputable financial firms with terrific products advertise, the firms that spend the most on advertising often are the ones with inferior offerings. Being bombarded with ads whenever you listened to the radio, watched television, or read magazines and newspapers was bad enough, but now email boxes, websites, and social media platforms are stuffed full of spam and promos, too.

WARNING

Responding to ads usually is a bad financial move, regardless of whether the product being pitched is good, bad, or so-so, because the company placing the ad typically is trying to motivate you to buy a specific product. The company doesn't care about your financial alternatives, whether its product fits with your tax situation, and so on. Many ads try to catch your attention with the supposed tax savings that their products generate.

## Following advice from websites and publications

Articles on websites and in magazines, newspapers, newsletters, and so on can help you stay informed, but they also can cause you to make ill-advised financial moves that overlook tax consequences. Article writers have limited time and space and often don't consider the big picture or ways their advice can be misunderstood or misused. Even worse is that too many writers don't know the tax consequences of what they're writing about.

## Overspending

An important part of financial literacy is understanding how to make good tax decisions. Far too many tax guides go on and on and on, talking about this tax break and that tax break. The problem is that to take advantage of many of the best tax breaks, you need to have money to invest. When you spend all that you earn, you miss out on many terrific tax benefits. And the more you spend, the more taxes you pay, both on your income and on the purchases you make (through sales taxes).

Just like losing weight, spending less sounds good, but most people have a hard time budgeting their finances and spending less than they earn. Perhaps you already know where the fat is in your spending. If you don't, figuring out where all your monthly income is going is a real eye-opener. The task takes some detective work — looking through your credit card statements and your checkbook register to track your purchases and categorize your spending. Chapter 2 gets you started on the right foot with the basics of budgeting and tracking your spending.

## Financial illiteracy

Lack of personal finance education is at the root of most money blunders. You may not understand the tax system and how to manage your finances because you were never taught how to manage them growing up or in high school or college.

Financial illiteracy is a widespread problem not just among the poor and undereducated. Most people don't plan ahead and educate themselves with their financial goals in mind. People react — or, worse, do nothing at all. You may dream, for example, about retiring and never having to work again. Or perhaps you hope that someday you can own a house or even a vacation home in the country or by the shore.

You need to understand how to plan your finances so you can accomplish your financial goals. You also need to understand how the tax system works and how to navigate within it to work toward your objectives.

TIP

If you need more help with important personal financial issues, pick up a copy of the latest edition of my book *Personal Finance For Dummies* (Wiley).

IN THIS CHAPTER

» Seeking assistance from a qualified financial advisor

» Uncovering how financial advisors determine their fees

» Understanding the services a financial advisor provides

# Chapter 10
# Ten Questions to Ask Financial Advisors

Based on my experience as a financial counselor, I firmly believe that you are your own best financial advisor. However, I know that some people don't want to make financial decisions without getting assistance. Perhaps you're busy or simply can't stand making money decisions. You need to recognize that you have a lot at stake when you hire a financial advisor. Besides the cost of their services, which generally don't come cheap, you're placing a lot of trust in their recommendations. The more you know, the better the advisor you can hire and the fewer services you need to buy.

The following questions will help you get to the core of an advisor's competence and professional integrity. Get answers to these questions *before* you decide to hire a financial advisor.

## What Portion of Your Income Comes from Clients' Fees versus Commissions?

Asking this question first may save you the trouble and time of asking the next nine questions. The right answer is "100 percent of my income comes from fees paid by clients." Anything less than 100 percent means that the person you're speaking to is a salesperson with a vested interest in recommending certain strategies and products.

Sadly, more than a few financial advisors don't tell the truth. In one undercover investigation, about one-third of self-proclaimed fee-only advisors turned out to be brokers who also sold investment and insurance products on a commission basis.

How can you ferret these people out? Advisors who provide investment advice and oversee at least $100 million must register with the U.S. Securities and Exchange Commission (SEC); otherwise, they generally must register with the state that they make their principal place of business. They must file Form ADV, otherwise known as the Uniform Application for Investment Adviser Registration. This lengthy document asks for the following specific information from investment advisors:

- A breakdown of where their income comes from
- Relationships and affiliations with other companies
- Education and employment history
- The types of securities the advisory firm recommends
- The advisor's fee schedule

In short, Form ADV provides — in black and white — answers to all the essential questions. With a sales pitch over the phone or marketing materials sent in the mail, a planner is much more likely to gloss over or avoid certain issues. Although some advisors fib on Form ADV, most advisors are more truthful on this form than they are in their own marketing. You can ask the advisor to send you a copy of Form ADV. You can also find out whether the advisor is registered or has a track record of problems by calling the SEC at 800-732-0330 or by visiting its website at www.adviserinfo.sec.gov.

Many states require the registration of financial advisors, so you should also contact the department that oversees advisors in your state. Visit the North American Securities Administrators Association's website (www.nasaa.org) and click on the "Contact Your Regulator" link on the home page.

## What Portion of Client Fees Is for Money Management versus Hourly Planning?

The answer to how the advisor is paid fees provides clues as to whether they have an agenda to persuade you to hire them to manage your money. If you want objective and specific financial planning recommendations, give preference to advisors who derive their income from hourly fees. Many counselors and advisors call themselves "fee-based," which usually means that they make their living managing money for a percentage of assets managed.

If you want a money manager, you can hire the best quite inexpensively through a mutual fund. Or, if you have substantial assets, you can hire an established money manager.

## What Is Your Hourly Fee?

The rates for financial advisors range from about $100 per hour up to several hundred dollars per hour. If you shop around, expect to pay more for advisors located in high-cost-of-living areas. As you compare planners, remember that what matters is the total cost that you can expect to pay for the services you're seeking.

## Do You Perform Tax or Legal Services?

Be wary of someone who claims to be an expert beyond one area. The tax, legal, and financial fields are vast in and of themselves, and they're difficult for even the best and brightest advisor to cover well simultaneously.

One exception is the accountant who also performs some basic financial planning by the hour. Likewise, a good financial advisor should have a solid grounding in the basic tax and legal issues that relate to your personal finances. Large firms may have specialists available in different areas.

## What Work Experience and Education Qualifies You to Be a Financial Planner?

This question doesn't have one right answer. Ideally, a planner should have experience in the business or financial services field. Some say to look for planners with at least five or ten years of experience. I've always wondered how planners earn a living their first five or ten years if folks won't hire them until they reach these benchmarks! A planner should also be good with numbers, speak in plain English, and have good interpersonal skills.

Education is sort of like food. Too little leaves you hungry. Too much can leave you feeling stuffed and uncomfortable. And a small amount of high quality is better than a lot of low quality.

Because investment decisions are a critical part of financial planning, take note of the fact that the most-common designations of educational training among professional money managers are MBA (master of business administration) and CFA (chartered financial analyst). And some tax advisors who work on an hourly basis have the PFS (personal financial specialist) credential. The CFP (certified financial planner) credential is also popular among those with general financial training.

## Do You Carry Liability Insurance?

Some counselors may be surprised by this question or think that you're a problem customer looking for a lawsuit. On the other hand, accidents happen; that's why insurance exists. So if the planner doesn't have liability insurance, they've missed one of the fundamental concepts of planning: Insure against risk. Don't make the mistake of hiring them.

You wouldn't (and shouldn't) let contractors into your home to do work without knowing that they have insurance to cover any mistakes they make. Likewise, you should insist on hiring a planner who carries protection in case they make a major mistake for which they are liable. Make sure that they carry enough coverage given what they are helping you with.

## Can You Provide References from Similar Clients?

Take the time to talk to other people who have used the planner. Ask what the planner did for them and find out what the advisor's greatest strengths and weaknesses are. You can find out a bit about the planner's track record and style. And because you want to have as productive a relationship as possible with your planner, the more you find out about them, the easier it'll be for you to hit the ground running if you hire them.

Some financial advisors offer a "complimentary" introductory consultation. If an advisor offers a free consultation to allow you to check them out and it makes you feel more comfortable about hiring them, fair enough. But be careful: Most free consultations end up being a sales pitch for certain products or services the advisor offers.

The fact that a planner doesn't offer a free consultation may be a good sign. Counselors who are busy and who work strictly by the hour can't afford to burn an hour of their time for an in-person free session. They also need to be careful of folks seeking free advice. Such advisors usually are willing to spend some time on the phone answering background questions. They should also be able to send background materials by mail and provide references.

## Will You Provide Specific Strategies and Product Recommendations?

This is an important question. Some advisors may indicate that you can hire them by the hour. But then they provide only generic advice without specifics. Some planners even *double-dip* — they charge an hourly fee initially to make you feel like you're not working with a salesperson, and then they try selling commission-based products. Also be aware of advisors who say that you can choose to implement their recommendations on your own and then recommend financial products that carry commissions.

## How Is Implementation Handled?

Ideally, you should find an advisor who lets you choose whether you want to hire them to help with implementation after the recommendations have been presented to you. If you know that you're going to follow through on the advice and you can do so without further discussions and questions, don't hire the planner to help you implement their recommendations.

On the other hand, if you hire a counselor because you lack the time, desire, and/or expertise to manage your financial life in the first place, building implementation into the planning work makes good sense.

# Index

# C



# D

# E

# F



# G



# H

# I

# T



# U

# V



# W



# Y



# Z

# About the Authors

**Eric Tyson, MBA,** has been a personal financial writer, lecturer, and counselor for the past 25+ years. As his own boss, Eric has worked with and taught people from a myriad of income levels and backgrounds, so he knows the financial concerns and questions of real folks just like you.

After toiling away for too many years as a management consultant to behemoth financial-service firms, Eric decided to take his knowledge of the industry and commit himself to making personal financial management accessible to everyone. Despite being handicapped by a joint BS in Economics and Biology from Yale and an MBA from Stanford, Eric remains a master at "keeping it simple."

An accomplished freelance personal-finance writer, Eric is the author or coauthor of numerous other *For Dummies* national bestsellers on personal finance, investing, for seniors, and home buying and is a syndicated columnist. His *Personal Finance For Dummies* won the Benjamin Franklin Award for Best Business Book.

Eric's work has been critically acclaimed in hundreds of publications and programs, including *Newsweek*, the *Los Angeles Times*, the *Chicago Tribune*, *Kiplinger's Personal Finance Magazine*, the *Wall Street Journal*, Bottom Line Personal, as well as NBC's *Today* show, ABC, CNBC, PBS's *Nightly Business Report*, CNN, FOX-TV, CBS national radio, Bloomberg Business Radio, and Business Radio Network. His website is www.erictyson.com.

**Ray Brown** is a veteran of the real-estate profession with over four decades of hands-on experience. A former manager for Coldwell Banker Residential Brokerage Company, McGuire Real Estate, and Pacific Union GMAC Real Estate, as well as a founder of his own real-estate firm, the Raymond Brown Company, Ray is currently a writer, consultant, and public speaker on residential real estate topics.

On his way to becoming a real estate guru, Ray worked as the real estate analyst for KGO-TV (ABC's affiliate in San Francisco) and was a syndicated real-estate columnist for the *San Francisco Examiner*. For 16 years he hosted a weekly radio program, *Ray Brown on Real Estate*, for KNBR. In addition to his work for ABC,

Ray has appeared as a real-estate expert on CNN, NBC, CBS, and in the *Wall Street Journal* and *Time*.

That's all fine and good. Ray's three proudest achievements, however, are Jeff and Jared, his two extraordinary sons, and over 55 years of nearly always wedded bliss to the *always* wonderful Annie B. Jeff's wife, Genevieve, and his grandson, Aidan Joseph Brown, are a continuing delight. Jared wisely married Jennifer Kirby in 2013 to complete the Brown dynasty.

**Bob Carlson** is editor of the monthly newsletter and website, *Retirement Watch*. Bob also is chairman of the board of trustees of the Fairfax County Employees' Retirement System, which has over $4 billion in assets. He has served on the board since 1992. He was a member of the board of trustees of the Virginia Retirement System, which oversaw $42 billion in assets, from 2001 to 2005.

His latest book is *Where's My Money: Secrets to Getting the Most Out of Your Social Security* (Regnery). His prior books include *Invest Like a Fox . . . Not Like a Hedgehog* and *The New Rules of Retirement*, both published by Wiley. He has written numerous other books and reports, including *Tax Wise Money Strategies* and *Retirement Tax Guide*. He also has been interviewed by or quoted in numerous publications, including the *Wall Street Journal*, *Reader's Digest*, *Barron's*, *AARP Bulletin*, *Money* magazine, *Worth* magazine, *Kiplinger's Personal Finance* magazine, the *Washington Post*, and many others. He has appeared on national television and on a number of radio programs. He is past editor of *Tax Wise Money*. The *Washington Post* calls Bob's advice "smart . . . savvy . . . sensible . . . valuable and imaginative."

Bob has been a guest on many local and nationally syndicated radio shows.

Bob received his JD and an MS (in accounting) from the University of Virginia, received his BS (in financial management) from Clemson University, and passed the CPA exam. He also is an instrument-rated private pilot.

**Robert S. Griswold** is a successful real estate investor and active, hands-on property manager with a large portfolio of residential and commercial rental properties who uses print and broadcast journalism to bring his many years of experience to his readers, listeners, and viewers.

He is the co-author with Eric of the national best-seller *Real Estate Investing For Dummies*, and he is the author of *Mortgage Management for Dummies*, *Property Management For Dummies* and *Property Management Kit for Dummies*, and co-author of the *Landlord's Legal Kit For Dummies*. He has been the real estate expert for NBC San Diego, with a regular on-air live-caller segment since 1995. Robert was the host of a live weekly radio talk show, "Real Estate Today!," for nearly 15 years, and was also the columnist for the syndicated "Rental Roundtable" and "Rental Forum" columns. These columns have been published in 50+ major newspapers throughout the country, and Robert has been recognized twice as the number-one real-estate broadcast journalist in the nation by the National Association of Real Estate Editors.

Robert's educational background includes having earned three degrees all from the Marshall School of Business at the University of Southern California. His bachelor's degree is in Finance and Business Economics and Real Estate Finance.

He also has a Master of Business Administration in International Finance as well as Real Estate and Urban Land Economics, plus he earned an MSBA (second master's) in Real Estate Development. His real estate investing and managing professional designations include the CRE® (Counselor of Real Estate), the CPM® (Certified Property Manager), ARM® (Accredited Residential Manager), the RPA® (Real Property Administrator), the ACoM® (Accredited Commercial Manager), the CCIM® (Certified Commercial Investment Member), the GRI® (Graduate, Realtor Institute®), the PCAM® (Professional Community Association Manager), and CCAM® (Certified Community Association Manager).

Robert has been retained on more than 4,000 legal matters as an expert in the standard of care and custom and practice for all aspects of real-estate ownership, management, maintenance, and operations in both state and federal cases throughout the country. He is the president of Griswold Real Estate Management, Inc., managing residential, commercial, retail, and industrial properties throughout Southern California and Nevada.

**Margaret Atkins Munro, EA** (who answers to Peggy) is a tax advisor, writer, and lecturer with more than 40 years' experience in various areas of taxation and finance with a mission in life to make taxes understandable. Her practice is concentrated in the areas of family tax, small business, trusts, estates, and charitable foundations.

She is a graduate of The Johns Hopkins University and has also attended University College Cork (Ireland) and the Pontifical Institute of Mediaeval Studies in Toronto, and she feels that her ability to decipher the language in the Internal Revenue Code derives completely from her familiarity with a variety of obscure medieval languages.

Peggy is the author of *529 & Other College Savings Plans For Dummies*, and co-author of *Estate & Trust Administration For Dummies.* Since her move to Costa Rica, she has become more fluent in cross-border issues facing U.S. expatriots living all over the world. She speaks on a variety of tax-related topics and has given numerous interviews to the national and international print and radio media relating her expertise in tax issues, especially with regard to their effects on families. You can reach her through her website at www.taxpanacea.com.


## Publisher's Acknowledgments

**Executive Editor:** Steve Hayes

**Compilation Editor:** Colleen Diamond

**Project Editor:** Colleen Diamond

**Copy Editor:** Christine Pingleton

**Production Editor:** Saikarhtick Kumarasamy

**Cover Image:** Wiley